D1525789

UNEQUAL CARE

UNEQUAL CARE

A CASE STUDY OF
INTERORGANIZATIONAL
RELATIONS IN HEALTH CARE

MURRAY MILNER, JR.

NEW YORK
COLUMBIA UNIVERSITY PRESS
1980

Murray Milner, Jr. is Associate Professor of Sociology at the University of Virginia

Library of Congress Cataloging in Publication Data
Milner, Murray, Jr.
Unequal care.

Includes index.
1. Health facilities—Sociological aspects.
2. Interorganizational relations.   3. Health
facilities—United States—Affiliations.   4. Medical cooperation—United States.   5. Poor—Medical
care—United States.   I. Title.   [DNLM: 1. Community health services—Organization and administration.   2. Interinstitutional relations.   WA546
AA1 M65u]
RA965.M47   362.1'1'0973   80-15612
ISBN 0-231-05006-2

Columbia University Press
New York   Guildford, Surrey

Copyright © 1980 Columbia University Press
All rights reserved
Printed in the United States of America

FOR MY
FATHER AND MOTHER

CONTENTS

PREFACE

American society is a frustration and embarrassment to Marxist radicals and progressive reformers alike: it continues to avoid the predicted "inevitable" collapse, but it stubbornly resists attempts to reduce socioeconomic inequalities—in contrast to the significant if inadequate progress made in reducing racial and sexual inequalities. Literally millions still suffer physical deprivation and social degradation, not to speak of a group of very wealthy who are at best ostentatious and wasteful and all too frequently arrogantly selfish and irresponsible. In sum, neither radicals nor liberals have had their hopes fulfilled.

How has this balancing act been carried out? What are the social stabilizing mechanisms that avoid serious discontent by making significant reform seem on the horizon, but that result in relatively little objective change in the distribution of resources and power? I believe that the improvement of either a radical or liberal analysis of American society requires more attention to this question.

Reform efforts have tended to have two major goals. One is to bring about equality of opportunity. The other is to ensure that all citizens have a basic level of income and services—a level sufficiently high to provide everyone a "decent" way of life. Efforts to achieve the first goal have concentrated on the educational system; equality of opportunity has been the professed goal of both liberals and conservatives. In an earlier work[1] I identified the mechanisms operating in this sector to limit the impact of programs to increase these opportunities. In this book I turn my attention to the other key reformist strategy, the attempt to ensure everyone a minimum level of goods and services. This process is examined in the context of health care, a service that almost all would agree should not be denied those in real need. This book looks at the differences in the quality of urban health care institutions and at the attempts to improve the minimum level of care for poor people. It also considers the mechanisms that have limited such efforts. Finally the institutional context, which allows and supports both the reform efforts and the social mechanisms that thwart these efforts, is analyzed. The book does not deal with all aspects of the so-called health care "crisis," for example, "professional dominance" by doctors[2] or the ever-increasing demands for help with psychological and social problems, as well as medical care. I have taken these into account, but they are not systematically analyzed.

While the substantive focus of the book is on urban health care, the analytical focus is on interorganizational relationships. Increasingly organizations rather than individuals have become the key actors in our society. Therefore the need to understand the nature and structure of interaction between such units grows in importance and urgency. The theoretical focus, however, is on three theoretical questions that are relevant whether the actors are individuals, organizations, or some more complex unit such as the nation-state: (1) the nature and forms of coordination, (2) the determinants of social conflict and stalemate, and (3) the sources of social inequality. Obviously issues as broad and complex as these cannot be discussed comprehensively in a monograph on urban health care. Rather the intent is to show that contemporary social problems can be understood best when seen from the perspective of recurring theoretical issues.

University of Virginia,
Charlottesville, Virginia
August 1980

ACKNOWLEDGMENTS

This book had its beginning in a research proposal that Amitai Etzioni and I wrote. A number of years have passed but I am still indebted to him both for intellectual stimulation and moral support. The early stages of the study were funded by the National Institute of Mental Health through the Center for Policy Research.

I benefited greatly from numerous conversations with Robert Alford, Harry Greenberg, Roberto Kleinfeld, and Edward Lehman. Astrida Butners, Naomi Gerstell, Michael Perelman, and Mary Pockman participated in the data collection process. The concept of a satellite organization was first developed by Alvin Katz.

The people who have assisted me at various stage of the typing, revising, and editing are too numerous to name, but I am deeply in their debt.

At several different stages of the writing my colleagues Frank Arnhoff, Robert Bierstedt, Theodore Caplow, Robert Chamberlain, Burke Grandjean, and Gresham Sykes read all or parts of the manuscript and provided useful suggestions. I also benefited from the suggestions of a significant number of students who read and commented on various parts of the work.

I am particularly grateful for the detailed and thoughtful criticisms of Charles Perrow.

My daughter Helene, my wife, Sylvia, and Mr. W. R. Mobley have struggled valiantly to improve my prose. Mr. Leslie Bialler has been unusually devoted and skillful in guiding the manuscript through the editorial process.

Finally, I want to offer my thanks, gratitude and respect to the staff of the various institutions and to the people of Southside that were the subject of this study.

UNEQUAL CARE

PART I

Chapter One

THE GROUNDWORK

The following events occurred about twelve months apart in the same neighborhood of one of the largest metropolitan areas in the United States. They were reported by two different observers.

The [ambulance] attendant went to a [school] swimming pool and a child about nine years old had a laceration on his foot. The nurse there asked where the ambulance is from and they said "Johnson Hospital." The kid started screaming, "Johnson! I'm not going to Johnson! You're goin' to murder me there!" Since the child's mother wasn't there they took him to Johnson.

We drive down Main to a supermarket at 16th Street. At the entrance of the market two policemen help Mrs. Marcus, 61, a small, gray-haired woman into the ambulance. She's wincing with pain and hobbling as she moves to the side bench and sits down. "A box fell on her leg," one of the policemen tells Ike, who begins filling in a pink form. As Ike asks the woman questions, José pulls out and starts driving back up Main toward Johnson. I can't hear Mrs. Marcus over the noise as she talks to Ike, but suddenly Ike turns to José and says, "She wants to go to Mercy Hospital." José nods and turns right. Ike looks back to Mrs. Marcus. "You know, Mercy is very crowded today. You'll have to wait all day." Mrs. Marcus pulls back from Ike scared. "Oh, no please don't take me to Johnson, please," she says intensely. "I'll wait at Mercy." Ike just nods his head.[1]

INEQUALITY AND INTERORGANIZATIONAL RELATIONS

As these accounts illustrate, at least some people in major metropolitan cities perceive two different types of health care institutions. One set is seen as providing very low quality care, "care" that may even do more harm than good. Other institutions are viewed as relatively high quality health care organizations that, if not perfect, are greatly preferable to the low-status institutions. Although the differences in all cities may not be as great as those implied by these accounts, it is common for metropolitan areas to have low-status, usually municipal, hospitals and higher status, usually voluntary, hospitals. The distinction between them is apparently well known—even children and "little old ladies" are acutely aware of the differences.

High- and low-status hospitals are simply a part of the larger pattern of an unequal distribution of health services. As David Mechanic notes:

As medicine has demonstrated greater efficacy, all segments of the population have gained greater appreciation of the high standard of medical care possible in the United States. With heightened expectations the failure to find accessible and responsive services has become a bitter pill to swallow, especially among more deprived groups who see their difficulties as one more manifestation of their exclusion from the mainstream of American society. Innumerable studies support these perceptions by demonstrating that the poor have a greater prevalence of illness, disability, chronicity, and restriction of activity because of health problems than those of higher status and that they have less accessibility to many health services and receive lower quality care.[2]

The purpose of this book is not primarily to document that inequalities exist. Rather it is an attempt to understand the dynamics of one aspect of this pattern of inequality, the nature of interorganizational relationships between urban health care institutions.

Two sets of interrelated questions are addressed. The first set asks why institutions with apparently drastic variations in quality continue to exist in close geographical proximity. How do low-status institutions (that most people want to avoid) manage to stay in business—especially when they are only a few blocks away from high-status ones? Why do people—even some with money—wind up at such institutions? Or why do health authorities allow such drastic variations in the quality of health care institutions in the same neighborhood? The simple commonsense answer is that rich people go to high-status institutions and poor people go to low-status ones and each group gets the quality of services they are able to pay for. But as we shall see, while this is in part true, the situation is considerably more complex.

The second set of questions focuses on the nature of the relationships beween the various health institutions in urban settings. Are institutions in the same metropolitan neighborhood in competition with each other or do they cooperate and coordinate their activities? If they are in competition, how do the low-status institutions survive? If they cooperate, why and how? Assuming for the moment that such institutions might want to cooperate, we ask how they manage to coordinate their efforts. There are few formal structures for this, much less any overall authority structure.

The central premise of this book is that these two questions—why an unequal dual system of health care institutions persists, and how these institutions relate to each other—are two facets of the same issue. The inequalities in urban health care—both why they are as great as they are and why they are not even greater—cannot be adequately understood without analyzing interorganizational relationships. The reverse is also true; these relationships between health care institutions cannot be understood unless they are viewed in the context of interorganizational and societal inequality. The essence of the argument is this: given the present structure of American society, high-quality health institutions in large metropolitan settings must limit the demands placed on them to serve the poor people and to treat medically uninteresting cases. If they do not do this, the quality of the services they offer—and eventually their status—are likely to decline. Consequently, for high-status institutions to exist, there must also be low-status institutions to take on the unwanted functions and patients. Moreover, for reasons we take up later, it is not possible simply to officially create these two types of institutions and then let each set go its own way. Maintenance of this informal division of labor requires extensive interorganizational relationships, and in a sense coordination, between the two types of institutions. On the one hand these relationships are designed to ensure the continued eminence and dominance of the high-status institutions; on the other hand they must ensure the continued existence of low-status institutions and their ability to operate at some minimal level of acceptability. High-status institutions both help and exploit lower status ones. Low-status institutions are often virtually powerless and yet an essential part of the local health care system. The nature of these relations is summarized under the concept of *symbiotic inequality*. This book is about the nature and operation of these interorganizational relationships under conditions of symbiotic inequality and the broader pluralistic institutional context that permits and supports this structure of inequality and informal coordination.

REFORM AND SOCIAL CHANGE

The inequalities of urban health care and the nature of interorganizational relations, particularly the supposed "lack of coordination" between institutions, have by no means gone unnoticed. A number of attempts have been made to reduce the inequalities and to increase the efficiency of health care. But this leads us to the question of what impact these various reform efforts have had. After studying 11 different programs directed toward improving access to health care—including Medicaid, Medicare, and attempts to increase the number of physicians—Charles Lewis concludes:

The principal effect of most efforts to improve access to care in the past has been to translocate barriers from one area of the system to the other. When economic barriers become politically unacceptable, legislation is passed. When such legislation becomes financially unacceptable, financial barriers are partly reerected and others increased or created.[3]

This conclusion leads to a basic question: how general and at what level of social organization must changes occur to eliminate the dual system of health care and to make adequate care reasonably accessible to all?

Sociologists who have previously analyzed various aspects of health care come to quite varying conclusions about this issue. In *Health Care Politics* Robert Alford characterizes three different approaches to analysis of the health care crisis.[4] On the one hand the pluralists see an essentially sound system in need of incremental adjustment to improve the quality of care provided the poor; most physicians subscribe to this perspective. In contrast the bureaucratic perspective sees the need to weaken if not break the monopoly of physicians and to increase greatly planning and coordination through more centralized authority; most hospital administrators, health planners, and public health officials identify with this view.[5] Alford himself subscribes to what he calls the institutional or class perspective, which claims that little if anything can be done if the focus of change is only health care:

> . . . the institutional or class perspective holds [that America's] wealth is composed of a large fraction of useless production for conspicuous consumption, . . . its democratic political institutions conceal a fundamental lack of access to decision-making power by a large fraction of the population, . . . its egalitarian ideals are contradicted by sharp inequalities of status, power, and wealth. . . . the American dream conceals fundamental and increasingly obvious flaws in the basic capability of the institutions of the society to provide what its technology and productive capacity make possible for the population as a whole.[6]

He argues that what is required is a fundamental struggle to change American social institutions, requiring "a social movement and political leadership which is not yet visible."[7]

In contrast, in *The Growth of Bureaucratic Medicine*, David Mechanic makes relatively positive comments about pluralistic approaches and negatively characterizes analyses that assume the United States is controlled by some kind of power elite.[8] He then characterizes Alford's analysis as utopian.[9] He clearly does not accept Alford's contention that meaningful health care reform is unlikely short of transformation of our major political and economic institutions. According to Mechanic, "it is incorrect to assume that modifications of health organizations do not have important substantive consequences. Medical care has been undergoing continuing adaptation from a variety of interventions aimed at dealing with access, cost and quality."[10]

What is at stake here are two interrelated questions. How much social change is required to significantly improve the equity and efficiency of health care delivery? And at what levels of social organization must this change occur: at the level of individual health care organizations, at the level of regional or national networks of such organizations, or must we first transform core economic and political institutions?

There is no simple answer to these questions, and no one study will resolve the issue. But this study does two things in an attempt to grapple with these questions. First, one attempt at incremental reform in urban health care is analyzed in some detail: a program to provide additional services for poor people and reduce the disparities between the two halves of the system. Second, in analyzing both this specific reform ef-

fort and the structure of interorganization relations in general, I have interrelated several levels of analysis. More specifically I show that what
happens at a given health care institution is affected by the interorganizational network of which it is a part and that the network is in turn
shaped by the broader institutional norms and control structures operating at the societal level. Therefore the story that follows moves back and
forth between an analysis of relationships between specific health institutions and an analysis of broader institutional structures at the societal
level. No claim is made that this approach is unique or sufficient; it is,
however, a necessary if not sufficient condition for resolving the issue
raised by the conflicting conclusions of Alford and Mechanic.

SOME THEORETICAL ISSUES

While the immediate focus is on the organization of health care, on a
more abstract level the book also considers how the data and analysis
bear upon three fundamental problems in sociological theory: (1) how are
collective activities coordinated, (2) what produces social conflict, and (3)
what are the sources of social inequality?

With respect to the first question, markets, bureaucratic authority,
and pluralistic decision-making are usually considered as the primary alternative means of coordinating activities. This analysis does, however,
identify a number of other mechanisms that produce coordination,
broadly conceived. Moreover, I argue that they all rely on the same two
basic processes to simplify collective decision-making, namely, abstraction and inequality (defined later). The purpose of the analysis and the
core of this part of the theoretical argument is to show that a wide variety of coordination mechanisms can be systematically described and
analyzed with a limited and parsimonious set of theoretical concepts.

Interdependence can lead to conflict rather than coordination. Or another possible outcome of interdependence is neither coordination nor
conflict but stalemate or withdrawal. What are the conditions making
one of these outcomes more likely? Attempts to answer this question are
sometimes hampered by the vagueness of the concepts, especially the
concept of conflict. I argue that we must distinguish between conflicts of
interests and social conflict per se, that is, the mutual use of negative

sanctions. Conflicts of interest that cannot be resolved may lead to either stalemate or social conflict. Consequently, the analysis indicates some of the determinants of these alternative outcomes.

For some time sociologists have tried to explain inequality from one of two basic perspectives. The functional approach emphasizes that inequality is basically due to a consensus about the differences in the importance of various activities and to variations in the natural scarcity of personnel needed to perform these activities; activities generally judged most important and for which personnel are most scarce receive the highest rewards. In contrast, the conflict perspective holds that inequalities are rooted in coercion, deception, and manipulation and in the concentration of power that makes these possible; people who receive the greatest rewards do so primarily because they are able to intimidate or fool others. Elaborating on an argument of Lenski's,[11] I suggest that there is a third basis of distribution, need, and need is not reducible to either of the two perspectives—unless one makes their concepts so broad that they result in tautologies. The analysis shows how all three bases of distribution play an important role in the interorganizational network of urban health care.

AN ANALYTICAL FRAMEWORK

Each of these three questions focuses on a crucial sociological process, namely, coordination, conflict, and inequality. These processes are analyzed in the context of interorganizational relationships. That is, we ask, why are the activities of organizations A and B coordinated, while those of C and D are uncoordinated? Or why is the relationship between A and B characterized by equality and cooperation, while that between C and D is unequal and conflict ridden? But an even prior question is why is there any kind of social relationship between organization A and B, or C and D? Stated another way our problem is to explain why some organizations are linked and others are not and why the links that do exist vary with respect to their degree of coordination, conflict, and inequality.

In explaining these differences in interorganizational relationships I consider three sets of factors: (1) resource dependencies and needs, (2) the time and energy required to negotiate the terms of a relationship, and (3) the institutionalized norms concerning such relationships. Perhaps these distinctions can be most easily communicated by illustrating their significance for an important type of interpersonal relationship. Whether one is married is affected by (1) one's need for companionship with the opposite sex, (2) the ease of negotiating an agreement to get married, and (3) the normative emphasis that one's particular culture places on being married. No one of these factors adequately explains why a given individual gets married, much less why he or she marries a particular person. The same is true with respect to interorganizational relationships. The analysis that follows considers all three influences. It does not, however, measure precisely the relative effect of each; the type of data used in this study makes this impossible. Rather I identify examples of each type of factor at work and, to some degree, indicate how they interact with each other. The second and third sets of factors are taken up in later chapters. The dominant theoretical orientation in the study of interorganizational relationships has focused on resource dependencies. At this point we need to consider the concepts and ideas central to this perspective.

RESOURCE DEPENDENCE:
INTERDEPENDENCE, SCARCITY, AND UNCERTAINTY

Much of interorganizational theory—and social theory in general—revolves around two central assumptions. First, actors, and especially organizations, usually prefer autonomy to dependence or interdependence, all other things being equal.[12] For example, organizations like to have direct control over resources and activities central to their well-being rather than be dependent on outside agents for these needs. But all other things are seldom equal, and this brings us to the second assumption. The main factor overriding the preference for autonomy is scarcity of some important resources. Stated another way, most interdependence is rooted in scarcity in at least two ways.

First and most directly, scarcity forces actors to compete with each other, and this leads to some form of interaction, for example, competition in the marketplace, dodging each other on a crowded sidewalk, debates during political campaigns. All are examples of interdependence emerging out of competition during the distribution process. Most, though not all, social conflict results from this source.

A second form of interdependence occurs in production. Instead of simply competing for what is available, actors decide to cooperate to increase their resources through joint production activities. This does not mean all benefit equally, or even that everyone participates voluntarily. But in contrast to the first type of interdependence, at least some parties deliberately attempt to increase interdependence and interaction in the hope of increasing productivity and thereby reducing scarcity. Generally, joint activity is more probable if each party brings to the task something the other does not have. Stated another way, cooperation in production, that is, joint activity, is most likely if there are both a common scarcity and complementary resources useful in reducing that scarcity.

Interdependence and loss of autonomy are particularly troublesome when accompanied by uncertainty. Dependency on other actors for one's vital resources is bad enough, but if the behavior of those actors is erratic and unpredictable, such dependency borders on the intolerable. Consequently, high interdependence produces a strong proclivity for ordered and stabilized relationships. Not infrequently actors are willing to sacrifice even additional autonomy if uncertainty can be reduced.

Previous analyses of interorganizational relationships have stressed the importance of scarcity, interdependence, and uncertainty as key variables. Benson, Aldrich, and especially Pfeffer and Salancik are associated with this perspective, though in some respects their approaches are quite different.[13] In their recent work Pfeffer and Salancik have shown that an impressive variety of phenomena—organizational growth, mergers, joint programs, interlocking boards of directors, cartels, trade associations, government regulation of industries, executive succession, and interorganizational exchange of personnel—can be analyzed and understood from this perspective. But while the array of phenomena included is impressive, the strength of the relationships between resource dependency variables and the formation of interorganizational relationships is often less impressive. In the language of statistics the relationships are statistically significant, but the vast proportion of the variance remains unexplained. This observation does not denigrate the very real accomplishments of the perspective but only indicates that a more nearly complete explanation probably requires the analysis of other kinds of variables.

A second shortcoming this perspective sometimes manifests is an overstatement of the tendency toward aggrandizement; one is sometimes reminded of a Darwin–Spencer imagery of survival of the fittest. For example, Benson says, "Cooperative strategies are limited to situations in which each party has some minimal degree of power vis-à-vis other parties. Each party must hold something of value for the other party and be capable of resisting the others' demands."[14] Such statements are not incorrect, but without careful specification and qualification they miss some of the subtleties involved in resource dependencies and power relations. For this reason we pay special attention to what I call *symbiotic inequality:* relationships wherein powerful, rich, and high-status institutions are engaged in significant cooperation with institutions that have virtually no power over them and offer no direct service in any conventional sense of these terms. Again the intent is not to reject the resource dependency perspective but to refine it. In addition, two more sets of factors mentioned earlier are used to supplement the perspective.

DATA AND METHODOLOGY

The core of the analysis in this book is based on a case study of a particular set of organizations in one urban neighborhood of one metropolitan city. The case study is based on direct observation, analysis of organizational records, numerous informal conversations with informants, and seventy relatively lengthy interviews with key informants. The more formal interviews were tape recorded and transcribed. Most of these were with health institution staff members who were particularly knowledgeable about the local network of interorganizational relationships. I personally conducted about one-third of the formal interviews and most of the informal ones. The others were conducted by research assistants working under my direction. During the data collection period, 1970–72, I lived in the neighborhood and my family received health care services from several of its institutions. I was an inpatient in one of the neighborhood hospitals for more than a week.

This type of more qualitative, informal methodology has not been characteristic of the seminal works on interorganizational relationships; these have tended to rely on survey research techniques. The work of Levine and White, Litwak and Hylton, Aiken and Hage, Turk, and to a lesser extent the early work of Warren, exemplify this approach.[15] This is in contrast to much of the seminal work in intraorganizational analysis, which often relied on case studies using qualitative methods. Alvin Gouldner's *Patterns of Industrial Bureaucracy*, Peter Blau's *The Dynamics of Bureaucracy,* and Philip Selznick's *TVA and the Grassroots* are three obvious examples.[16] Consequently not only because of cost and convenience factors but also because of the fruitfulness of case studies in intraorganizational analysis and the dominance of quantitative work in interorganizational analysis I decided to undertake a case study relying primarily on qualitative methods that would attempt to relate the case study to higher levels of social organization.

After the data collection was completed Roland Warren and his associates[17] suggested a more systematic rationale for such an approach drawn from the perspective of the sociology of knowledge. Their concerns and conclusions are directly related to the disagreement between Alford and Mechanic: how much change has occurred and can occur in the health care sector without changing more basic institutional structures? At the risk of considerable oversimplification, we can say that sociology of knowledge sees ignorance (or its obverse, knowledge) and interests as inextricably intertwined. What one knows to be "true" is to a significant degree dependent on one's position in the social structure and the interests associated with that position. Just as various subgroups have different interests and goals, they also have different knowledge. Carried to the extreme, this argument lapses into complete relativism and subjectivism, but it is a useful critique of the naive view that assumes the existence of an unproblematic objective reality.[18]

Roland Warren has emphasized what has been a more secondary theme by turning the issue around. His concern is not so much how the position of the observer influences what is seen and known but rather how the level of social organization examined influences the selection of methodologies and what is seen.[19] Whether one understands social problems as primarily ignorance to be solved by incremental reforms or as primarily conflicting interests to be solved by more fundamental political change depends, in part, on whether one looks at the micro or macro level of analysis. In this context micro level means looking at single pairs of organizations one at a time, while macro means looking at a larger set of organizations as an interrelated system. More specifically, Warren's argument refers to how the level of interorganizational relations that are the focus of analysis—individual transactions, pair relationships, organizational sets, or entire networks—affects the conclusions. Looking at the micro level, one may see what appear to be high levels of interaction, coordination, conflict, and innovation. From this level of analysis one might conclude that considerable change is already taking place and that it is ridiculous to argue that nothing can be done without fundamental political change. When these same micro outcomes are viewed from a macro perspective, however, these dynamic processes may seem to have little effect on the broader structure. It may very well appear that all the reform programs, conflict, and change at the micro level are really much ado about not much in the way of broader structural change. Moreover, a focus on the micro level is likely to lead to an emphasis on quantitative methodologies, while a focus on more macro structures usually involves less precise, interpretative strategies. (This is true if only because by definition there are far fewer comparable macro units available to analyze. In the United States there are millions of patients, thousands of health care organizations such as hospitals, but only one national "system.")[20] Stated another way, the level of social organization on which one's analysis focuses is not only a substantive choice determined by research interest but also to some degree a methodological and ideological choice. Even if one does not advocate anything but directs one's analysis solely to description and explanation,[21] what one chooses to study has political implications. The selection of levels of analysis, micro or macro, is one aspect of this more general problem.

In part the heavy reliance on quantitative methodology for the study of interorganizational relations was due to greater emphasis on quantitative methods in the social science disciplines as whole. But it seems worth noting that most of this interorganizational research was funded by government agencies more interested in policy recommendations relevant to incremental administrative decisions than in fundamental political change. To point this out is not to denigrate this work or quantitative methodologies, much less the motives of the investigators or even the conscious intent of funding agencies. Warren's own research and the initial stages of this present study were also funded by such agencies. Nonetheless it does suggest that Warren's thesis may have some merit if not pushed too far.

All of this is to suggest that, quite apart from cost and convenience, case studies of interorganizational relationships using largely qualitative methodologies may make contributions in addition to those made by quantitative analyses. Moreover, it would seem important to focus such a study on both the micro and macro level and to interrelate the two. The present study makes this effort. One consequence is that the analysis goes far beyond the actual data collected. Arguments about the macro institutional structures are interpretations of readings and general observations as much as they are inferences from the data. Consequently the conclusions drawn from this process are necessarily quite tentative. This is a tolerable limitation, one hopes, since the purpose of a case study is not to verify propositions but to suggest new perspectives for analyzing subsequent data.

Those who have a proclivity for rigor and precision will think that I have carried the interpretative process too far. Those who believe that all significant issues must be analyzed in relation to the total "concrete" system, and especially in relation to an analysis of the class structure, will think that I have stopped short. To some degree both are correct. I can only hope that they will carry on where I have left off.

Chapter Two

THE NEIGHBORHOOD
HEALTH SYSTEM

THE SETTING AND THE ACTORS

The setting is a neighborhood in one of the large metropolitan areas of the United States. I shall call the city Fairmont and the neighborhood the Southside.* Actually, what is referred to as the Southside is more than a neighborhood but less than the south side of the city. It includes a number of smaller subneighborhoods such as Heightsville, Ricker's Hill, Bayside, and Queensborough. The population of the Southside is quite mixed with respect to socioeconomic, racial, and ethnic composition, though usually a particular subneighborhood is relatively homogeneous. On the whole the area is considered respectable but not fashionable. Its elite are for the most part intellectuals and politicians rather than the rich.

To the west of Southside is Wattsbury, the city's largest black ghetto. To the east and south is a large lake that effectively isolates the Southside from the populated areas on the other side, which at any rate are in a different political jurisdiction. Immediately to the north is a mixture of residential, business, and commercial areas. Eventually the business and commercial buildings predominate and become the heart of the downtown area.

---

* All names are pseudonyms in order to ensure the confidentiality of the informants.

In many respects the Southside is representative of the nation's most urbanized middle-class areas. It certainly has many blighted and segregated pockets and is adjacent to the city's main black ghetto, but it manages to maintain a precarious identity and quality of its own.

A word is necessary about the boundaries of the Southside and their significance for our study. There are no formal delineations for either the subneighborhoods or the Southside. To select the initial focal organizations, a demarcation line was drawn following key ecological barriers wherever possible. Approximately 25 health-care facilities fall within our semiarbitrary boundaries. Three general hospitals are located in the neighborhood. There are five homes for the aged with significant health care facilities and two commercial nursing homes. Fairmont municipal district health station and a branch station are included, as well as a comprehensive health care program for the poor that operates within the health station building. The other health facilities are a variety of client service organizations, including a psychological counseling center, several service programs for older persons, and various satellites of the larger institutions such as a methadone maintenance center operated by one of the hospitals. This particular area has fewer major health institutions than many parts of the city. However, it contains a considerable variety of such institutions, and these represent most of the major types of organizations involved in networks of health care facilities.

We shall not consider all the health care institutions in the Southside; rather, we shall focus on what are perhaps the four most important institutions: a low-quality voluntary hospital, a low-quality city hospital, a high-quality voluntary teaching hospital, and a new "experimental" comprehensive health care center. The first two institutions allow us to look for links among those institutions supposedly most in need of cooperative efforts. When these institutions are compared and related to the high-quality hospital, we get a look at the links that develop across the existing dual system: a system for the poor and a system for the upper and middle classes. The fourth institution represents an attempt to provide high-quality care to the poor by linking together the teaching hospital and a neighborhood council representing the poor. It is an example of one of the many attempts to reform the obvious inadequacies of the present dual system.

JOHNSON HOSPITAL

"This is the shithouse, and that's the glamour joint." That was the way one employee of Johnson Hospital compared it to Mercy Hospital. Unfortunately this characterization was not simply hyperbole. Johnson, a small voluntary hospital, is one of the poorest hospitals in the city. Immediately to the west is the city's vast black ghetto. To the east is an area that is fast developing into a Spanish-speaking ghetto. Like many of the buildings in the neighborhood, the hospital is old and in bad repair, and remodeling is economically impractical.

Because the hospital is voluntary and of low status, attempts to raise money for a new building have been unsuccessful. So, for more than 20 years the building, the facilities, and the quality of the care have continued to deteriorate.

The vast majority of its doctors, and all of its house staff, are foreign trained and by prevailing standards in the city are considered to be poorly qualified. Very few of them have or would be able to obtain appointments at major teaching hospitals, though, as we shall see, there are a few notable exceptions.

Johnson has not always been in such a desperate and unenviable position. Its history is long and respectable, if not prestigious. But since at least World War II there has been a steady downhill trend. In the last decade Johnson's financial condition has become critical and has gone through an endless series of crises. On several occasions the hospital seemed almost certain to close. The hospital must generally pay cash in advance for medicines and supplies because of delays in meeting earlier bills. Frequently, basic medicines and supplies are scarce or even unavailable because there is no money to purchase them. The building, facilities, and the small endowment are mortgaged to the limit. Often it is not even clear whether the hospital can meet its next payroll.

That Johnson has continued in operation is little short of miraculous. Yet, somehow, it has managed to hang on through crisis after crisis. Rumors circulate that the city and state governments have on occasion provided unannounced contributions to prevent Johnson's closure. Supposedly such support is motivated by a desire to avoid the political consequences of closing a hospital in an area already suffering from a scarcity of health care facilities and personnel. If such support occurred, it remained unannounced, probably to avoid establishing a precedent, since many hospitals in the city have severe financial problems. But clandestine rescue efforts have not been the primary reason for Johnson's survival. The main survival factor seems to have been the extraordinary set of interorganizational relationships created to secure and stretch the hospital's resources.

MERCY HOSPITAL

Founded in 1850 Mercy Hospital is 10 or 15 years older than Johnson Hospital, and is located about a mile north of it. In the past, Mercy was to some extent under the control of the officials of a religious denomination. In more recent years virtually all formal and legal ties have been severed. However, many informal ties remain and the influence of this religious association is still apparent. The hospital is located in a middle-class neighborhood not far from a large university. The boundaries between this neighborhood and the ghetto are not far away, and in recent years "security" has increasingly been a problem.

Mercy is without question a high-quality, high-status hospital, though a few hospitals in the metropolitan area are more prestigious. A partial affiliation with University Medical School has been maintained for more than fifty years, and residency training programs exist in most of the specialty fields. The majority of the staff, residents, and interns come from the best medical schools. Patients come from all over the city and even from out of the state to be treated, though the vast majority of patients are from the Southside and adjoining areas.

A dozen large buildings, within a two-block area house most of Mercy's programs. The majority of the buildings are relatively modern; one is brand new. The older buildings are stately and well kept. The hospital has a number of humanizing auxiliary services: a recreation department, professional counseling, regular worship services, and frequent musical concerts open to patients and staff. For inpatients, especially private patients, Mercy is a nice place to be if one has to be sick.

The outpatient department (OPD) is another matter. The technical quality of the medical care is probably quite good on the average, but the human quality leaves much to be desired. The system is fragmented, bureaucratized, and impersonal. The department is divided into an amazing number of specialty clinics, many of which are available only a few hours a week. The procedures often involve waiting in line and can be very frustrating for the patients. On his first visit the patient must go through a long registration process and be issued a clinic card; this card is a prerequisite to any treatment. Registration includes disclosure of income, since fees are scaled accordingly.

Before the patient can see a physician he must go to the cashier and pay for the scheduled appointment. Frequently there is a long line at the cashier's window. Almost without exception these contacts are abrupt and cursory. The patient then proceeds to the particular specialty clinic to which he has been assigned and waits for his name to be called. Often this involves more waiting. Eventually the patient is placed in an examination room, and frequently still more waiting follows. Finally he is examined by the doctor, usually a resident in training at the hospital. If the doctor orders any kind of test not covered by the initial fee—even a urinalysis—the patient must return to the cashier's window and pay for the service and then return to the clinic. Of course more elaborate tests like x-rays or scanning require trips to other parts of the hospital and possibly even a separate appointment. If drugs are prescribed this requires waiting at still another window. Mercy is no worse than the OPDs at most large hospitals and better than some, but nonetheless one is often subjected to a frustrating and dehumanizing experience.

If the story of Johnson Hospital is one of long-term decline and deterioration, Mercy is just the opposite. Clearly since World War II the hospital has grown tremendously in size, quality, and status. Until the last few years there was every indication that the trend would continue. However, the financial squeeze that has hit most hospitals has left the future clouded to say the least, and one senses uncertainty and even pessimism among many associated with Mercy.

BERNSTEIN HOSPITAL

About halfway between Mercy and Johnson, just into the edge of the black ghetto of Wattsbury, is Bernstein Hospital. In terms of size and quality it is very much like Johnson. If anything, the physical plant is in worse condition, though remodeling is now under way. Two things distinguish Bernstein from Johnson Hospital.

First Bernstein is clearly "over the line" into Wattsbury, and most of its patients, staff, and administration are black. Johnson, of course, treats many blacks and has many blacks on the staff, but other ethnic minorities and poor people also make up a significant portion of both its staff and patients. Bernstein is not a racist institution that discriminates against non-Negroes, but there is a significant difference in "ethnic atmosphere." Johnson is a poor peoples' institution; Bernstein is a black peoples' institution. In Fairmont it is hard to be a poor peoples' institution without being in part a black institution, and even more difficult to be a black institution without being a poor one. The second and more important difference is that Bernstein is a unit of the larger municipal system rather than an independent voluntary hospital. Most of the staff and administrators are to some degree city bureaucrats—in a technical, not necessarily a pejorative sense. This has two significant implications that further distinguish Bernstein from Johnson. While resources are almost as scarce as they are at Johnson, they are more certain. Every year the city's budget does commit a certain amount of money to Bernstein's operation. The second important consequence of being a city institution is that Bernstein relies primarily on other city hospitals for backup services, whereas Johnson must create its own network.

Until recently Johnson and Bernstein were very similar with respect to the scope and quality of the facilities or services, except that Bernstein provided obstetrical services and Johnson did not. Two things have happened to give Bernstein a significant edge in some respects. First, a new comprehensive family care center has been opened in a facility not far from the main building. The center is new and attractive and offers comprehensive care to ambulatory patients; this relieves the pressure and overcrowding at the Bernstein emergency room. Second, Bernstein is undergoing badly needed remodeling. Although this remodeling will for the most part simply bring the hospital facilities up to minimal standards, the change will be a big improvement.

THE DUAL SYSTEM

The contrast between Johnson and Bernstein on the one hand, and Mercy, on the other hand, represents the single most striking feature about the health care system of the Southside and Fairmont in general: one system of facilities for the poor and another for those who are more affluent or who have adequate health insurance. Increasingly the city's medical system has been characterized by a set of high-status teaching hospitals and a set of low-status institutions. Undoubtedly the correlation between status and the technical quality of the medical care is real but imperfect. But whatever the objective quality, city hospitals like Bernstein and the low-status voluntaries like Johnson have a reputation among the middle and upper classes as places to be avoided. In fact this reputation is also widespread among the poor.

The duality of the system should not be overstated. Most of the high-quality institutions treat large numbers of low-income patients. This leads us, however, to the second main structural feature of the dual system: the high-status institutions are internally stratified. That is, they have one type of service for the "private patients" who are able to pay the full cost of their care and another type of service for those who cannot. When the latter are admitted to the hospital, they are "ward patients"; when they are treated as ambulatory cases, they are "clinic patients." The critical division between the high-status and the low-status institutions is not that one treats poor patients. Rather only the high-status institutions treat significant numbers of well-to-do private patients. Equally important the higher status institutions are usually able to limit the number of poor patients treated so that the needs and demands of these patients do not overwhelm the available facilities, staff, and resources.

As alluded to in the description of Mercy the ward patients at the voluntary hospitals usually receive reasonably humane treatment, whereas the outpatient departments are often very little better than those of the lower status institutions. The reason is rather obvious: most individuals are entitled to some type of third-party payment for inpatient care. Even many of the poor are covered by Medicaid, and the elderly, whether rich or poor, have Medicare. Therefore high-status institutions can manage to avoid the worst aspects of bureaucratized impersonal care for inpatients, but this is much less so with respect to outpatients.

In Johnson Hospital all patients having Medicaid are treated as private patients; that is, they may choose to be treated by any doctor associated with the hospital. To the extent that the staff's poor reputation and low status are warranted such choice is a rather nominal privilege. Medicaid coverage does not entitle one to even such symbolic privileges at Mercy. In short, the poor at Mercy are the rich at Johnson.

This duality of the hospital system has been paralleled by an increasing duality in the type of primary care received. Over the years fewer and fewer physicians have opened private offices in the Southside neighborhood. More significantly, the trend toward specialization has meant fewer and fewer family doctors or general practitioners. The specialists, even internists and pediatricians, tend to be associated with the higher status hospitals and charge fees that lower income groups simply cannot afford. The result has been an increasing segregation of the well-to-do who can afford the fees of private physicians from those who cannot. The latter have come to rely more and more on the outpatient departments and the emergency rooms of the local hospitals for their ambulatory care. The expanding demand on these facilities has resulted in the overcrowded, bureaucratized conditions described earlier.

PART II

Chapter Three

A CENTRALIZED AUTHORITY
STRUCTURE

When the analytical framework was discussed in chapter 1, I indicated that we would draw on three sets of factors to explain interorganizational relationships: resource dependencies, the time and energies required to negotiate the terms of a relationship, and the norms of the institutional context governing relationships between organizations. In the next three chapters we focus primarily on the second set of factors. Each of these chapters discusses a different type of mechanism used to simplify negotiation: centralized authority structures, quasi-markets, and pluralistic decision-making. But before we turn to the analysis of a centralized authority structure in the neighborhood health system, it is necessary to introduce some rather abstract theoretical concepts. These concepts will enable us to organize the data presented in these three chapters within a common framework and to show that centralized authority, markets (and quasi-markets), and pluralistic decision-making are all variations on a common set of social processes.

SIMPLIFICATION OF DECISION-MAKING
AND COORDINATION

One type of interdependence is joint productive activity. Joint activity involves two basic processes: (1) decision-making and coordination—ac-

complished primarily through social interaction—and (2) actually producing the desired goods or services—accomplished by activity. Generally speaking, the more time spent on interaction to make decisions and
coordinate activities, the less time is available for productive work and
activity. All goal-oriented groups face this recurrent dilemma. How
much time and energy should be spent on deciding what to do and how
to do it as opposed to actual production? If inadequate resources are invested in coordination, production is reduced because individual efforts
are not mutually supportive, or they even hamper each other. On the
other hand, production can easily be reduced by overly elaborate and
costly planning and coordination schemes.

The most rudimentary means of coordination is *particularistic interaction:* all the relevant actors discuss, argue, and even fight until a set of
mutual expectations emerges based on some combination of consensus or
dominance among the actors.[1] But when actors do not have previously
established relationships, coordination based on particularistic interaction is very time-consuming. Because of this we often hear complaints
about the time "wasted" when the members of a committee must hammer out a consensus before a collective decision can be made.

A note about terminology is required. Up to this point I have used the
word "coordination." This term implies that things are fit together by
conscious planning. Often, however, activities are interrelated by unconscious and even unintended processes. The most obvious example is the
"invisible hand" of Adam Smith's competitive market. Consequently I
use "integration" to refer to this general fitting together process. Coordination then is one way to integrate activity.[2]

Because of the large amounts of time required to coordinate activities
by particularistic interaction most groups seek ways to simplify the process of collective decision-making and integration. That is, they seek to
establish *simplification mechanisms.* Two rudimentary processes are involved in all attempts to simplify collective decision-making. The first is
the development of mutually shared *abstractions.* A common language is
the most obvious example. But sets of mutual understandings, expectations, norms, rules, and laws are examples more relevant to our concerns. If we have a rule that we work from eight in the morning to five in
the afternoon, Monday through Friday, we do not have to spend time ar-

guing about whether the present moment should be used for work or recreation. We need only to know what day and time it is to reach such a decision; we can ignore many other factors such as whether it's a nice day, or we are in the mood, or there is a good movie on. We have abstracted out two characteristics that allow us to make a collective decision quickly; if it is between eight and five on a weekday we should be at work. The second basic simplification process is *inequality* of power; some individual or subgroup of the total collectivity is able to decide for the group as a whole and enforce their decision on the other members. Such inequality may be supported by the group as a whole, as when we decide to elect a president of a voluntary association, or may be imposed by violence, as in the case of a slave plantation. In contrast to abstractions, which simplify by reducing the number of factors to be taken into account, inequality simplifies by reducing the number of different actors participating in the decision-making.

Perhaps the most elemental simplification mechanism is the establishment of a *particularistic relationship*. We have worked together before and we know what to expect from each other. That is, we have established abstract mutual expectations that help us predict each other's behavior, and this in turn helps integrate any future activity. From our past experience together patterns of dominance emerge: one of us is usually more competent, or stronger, or more persuasive. Since we know who is likely to win future arguments or battles we usually follow the preferences of the dominant member of the group. Because of our shared abstractions (in the form of mutual expectations) and inequality of power (in the form of informal dominance) less time is needed for the group to make decisions or integrate subsequent activities. Our established relationships reduce the amount of interaction required to integrate any additional joint activity.

But particularistic relationships require a past history of common experience. In a highly mobile, heterogeneous society with high levels of complex productive activity, well-established particularistic relationships cannot be the sole or even primary means of simplification. Consequently, many additional more complex and formal mechanisms of simplification have been evolved. The two most important ones are centralized authority structures (particularly bureaucracies) and competitive

markets.[3] At a later point we take up how these more complex simplification mechanisms can also be conceptualized as being dependent on
various forms of abstraction and inequality.

Earlier work has dealt tangentially with various aspects of simplification. Domain consensus—general agreement about the primary functions, activities, and rights of each organization—has long been considered an important prerequisite to cooperative interorganizational
relationships.[4] Litwak has emphasized the significance of activities' being
uniform enough so that they can be regulated by standardized abstractions.[5] Hall has noted the importance of what I called particularistic interpersonal relationships for interorganizational coordination.[6] Benson
points out the significance of various kinds of consensus and mutual respect, though he argues that these aspects of the "superstructure" are ultimately determined by resource dependencies.[7] In short, previous work
has not completely ignored the factors influencing how easy or difficult it
is to negotiate and establish a working relationship—the assumption
being that a need for resources provides a motivation for doing so. But
for the most part these factors have been treated in a relatively ad hoc
fashion. The following analysis places these individual processes in a
more systematic framework to show that they are different facets of a
more general process. The goal is to provide a synthesis for simplification, paralleling to some degree the synthesis Pfeffer and Salancik have
provided for the resource dependency approaches.

A CENTRALIZED AUTHORITY STRUCTURE

The remainder of this chapter describes and analyzes a single centralized
authority structure. Bureaucratic centralized authority is relatively rare
in the interorganizational networks of urban health care systems. They
are, however, the most familiar means of simplification and therefore the
place to begin the analysis. Centralized authority, that is, inequality of
power, reduces the number of actors participating in decision-making.
But those at the top of a large hierarchy cannot be every place at once to
decide each and every case. Therefore, they create abstractions, for example, rules to guide their subordinates. This combination of inequality

and abstraction is particularly effective when large numbers of relatively routine and standardized decisions must be made quickly.

To illustrate and analyze this type of simplification mechanism, we shall focus on the ambulance system. It is directed by a city agency and coordinated through a highly developed communications system. Johnson Hospital is the Southside's key actor in the ambulance system, but as we shall see, this service has important consequences for nearly all Southside institutions and for the structure of the neighborhood health care system.

VIEW FROM THE TOP

Let us begin our analysis of Johnson's ambulance service with an official description of the larger city ambulance system and Johnson's relationship to it. This is what Donald Kaufmann, director of the City Ambulance Service (CAS), told us:

This office is primarily responsible for ambulances. . . . We run, depending on the time of day, anywhere from 60 to 80 ambulances. Approximately two-thirds of these ambulances are operated directly by us; one-third are operated by voluntary hospitals under contract with us. For instance, we have a contract with Johnson Hospital for a certain amount of money. . . . This contract means they run three ambulances around the clock. We are responsible for giving them calls. We are responsible for seeing what they are supposed to be doing. We do not have jurisdiction over the employees per se because they work for the hospital. If there is a problem with one of their employees we refer it to the hospital; we do not handle it ourselves.

The lower Southside is served by the three ambulances operated from Johnson Hospital. The patients picked up by ambulance in this area are returned to Johnson Hospital for the most part, although a certain number of patients are dropped off at Mercy Hospital. Patients are dropped off probably because of preference or clinic registration at Mercy. Or they are a serious case when the ambulance crew doesn't want to go the extra distance to Johnson, so they are dropped off at Mercy. . . . Johnson does approximately 18,000 calls a year, which is busy, but is not any busier than any other ambulance area in the city for the most part. . . . In terms of the quality of their work . . . they are pretty much average.

In Fairmont free ambulance service is available to anyone who calls a special emergency telephone number. The centralized dispatching service then assigns the first available ambulance in the vicinity of the call. Most of the time ambulances respond to calls within their specified geographical district. But if one district station has an excess of calls and another district within reasonable distance has a free ambulance, the call is assigned to the latter.

The police department had been dispatching ambulances, but this function was being transferred to CAS to reduce response time and to improve the screening of calls. Elaborate sets of procedural rules govern the assignment of ambulances. Supposedly, dispatchers who handled only ambulance calls and worked directly for CAS would better understand the complicated rules and do a more effective job of screening and dispatching.

VIEW FROM THE BOTTOM

To supplement Mr. Kaufmann's description let us turn to the account of an observer who spent a day on call with the Johnson Hospital ambulance crew and Bill Malacas, the head of that crew.[8]

The ambulance crews work out here, away from the stuffiness; the ambulances and the people [paying patients] they bring in . . . . about two-thirds of the hospital's patients—keep Johnson alive [financially solvent].

The phone rings, and someone from the card game jumps up to answer it. "That'll be an ambulance call," Malacas tells me, "so you better get ready to go." I ask him what type of calls they usually get. "Mostly, all the things that go with old age—heart problems, breathing, all that. But we also get plenty of stabbings and gunshot wounds." Malacas smiles. "The old people die naturally and the young ones kill each other."

As I head for the ambulances parked outside, he stops me, serious now. "You'll find most of the people we pick up won't want to come back here. They have that choice; we have to take them wherever they say. Mercy has to accept them now, by law; they didn't want to, they don't want to serve the community around them. Some people finally told Mercy to serve the community or they'll burn it down."

I jump into the ambulance as it starts to pull out, with José driving and Ike, the burly black man who won the poker hand, riding as the attendant. Michele, 19, a chubby volunteer health aide from a junior college, climbs into the truck after me.

As the truck turns onto the street, I ask Michele how she likes working at Johnson; I want to compare her reactions to mine. "Well," she almost shudders, "I wouldn't want to be brought here if I needed an ambulance. My friend was here once as a patient, and he says he saw roaches all over the place."

Ike is checking the supplies as we bounce down the street. I have to hang onto a pole in the truck to keep from slamming against the sides; even though we aren't going very fast, the ride is rough. A flashing red light revolves on the truck's roof, but I can't hear a siren. "It's burnt out," Ike explains, "and we don't have the money to fix it. The drivers usually fix their own trucks when they break down." I remember then the man working under the hood of one of the ambulances; he was a driver, not the mechanic I had taken him for.

Because the siren isn't working, we stop at a light; traffic is heavy and the cars, despite the ambulance's revolving light, won't move out of the way. "Hey, you see this," Ike turns to me, shouting over the engine noise. "Johnson has a bad reputation for taking a long time to get ambulances to calls. But it wouldn't matter much even if we had a siren on this truck; our sirens do work sometimes, and Fairmont drivers still don't get out of the way. The police let them get away with it—it's the only city it could happen in."

The first call took the ambulance crew to a junior high school. But the child was not as seriously injured as the school officials had thought, and ambulance transport was not needed. The crew checked in with Central Dispatch and went directly to their next call. They picked up a lady who insisted on being taken to Mercy. After that:

Another call crackles across the radio. José turns down Alexander to 19th, and pulls up before an apartment building. Ike jumps out and walks into the lobby, where Mr. Lindgren, 73, a thin, white-haired man, is sitting on some steps with two neighbors. "He feels dizzy and sick," one of them tells Ike. "He wants to go to County Hospital." Ike grunts, his disgust obvious; County is across town and the trip will take at least 15 minutes.

We help Mr. Lindgren into the ambulance and settle back for the ride. Ike looks troubled. "You know," he says to me, "I don't like it when people put down Johnson, like Michele did. Johnson isn't that bad, it's not so bad that everyone we pick up has to go to other hospitals. It's always those who can pay who go somewhere else, and we get the rest. But still," he says slowly, "I've been here three years, and, well . . . I'm not really jaded yet." He looks out the window as we stop again at a red light; the crosstown traffic is heavy.

Ike, late in the afternoon, sits quietly staring out of the ambulance window again, as we drive back to the garage. We have picked up six patients, but only one went to Johnson. Billy, a 13-year-old, broke his arm playing basketball. Ike didn't ask him where he wanted to go.

As this observer's account indicates, the ambulance service has its problems. As with most human institutions and organizations a considerable gap exists between the official description of how the system should work and what actually happens. In most respects the officials responsible for the system are aware of the discrepancies and are making efforts to solve the problems. But, despite undoubtedly genuine efforts, serious difficulties remain.

SOURCES AND BENEFITS OF CENTRALIZED AUTHORITY

The ambulance service illustrates well some of the gains and losses resulting from centralized bureaucratic coordination. Two key requirements of an emergency ambulance service in a metropolitan city are apparent: large numbers of decisions must be made and implemented very quickly, and each decision implementation needs to be coordinated with all others made within a given span of time. To obtain such an outcome through direct particularistic interaction would be very difficult. If each hospital operated its own ambulance service in a city the size of Fairmont the result would be near chaos, not to speak of the waste of duplication.[9] Even on the assumption that all hospitals agreed to coordinate their ambulance services and not compete with one another, how would this occur? In situations where many crucial, literally life and death, decisions must be made very quickly, a centralized authority structure is created to coordinate interorganizational activity—even in an institutional sector that has traditionally denied the legitimacy of such structures.

Four factors contribute to the need for a centralized authority: (1) the large number of decisions required, (2) the short time span in which the decisions must be made, (3) the potential life-and-death importance of the decision, and (4) the relatively standardized, universalistic nature of the decisions. This particular combination of structural pressures produces virtually the only legitimate exception to the general ideology of autonomy. (It might be argued that licensing and accrediting are vested in a centralized authority, but these functions for the most part involve decisions far removed from day-to-day operations and do not primarily focus on interorganizational coordination.)

The fourth factor, the standardized, uniform nature of the cases and the required decisions, is of special importance. Because these are standardized the primary organizational problem of the ambulance service appears to be communication of information rather than consensus formation. That is, there is little potential conflict between institutions over the day-to-day operational decisions that must be made to carry on this service. Consequently, the creation of this particular centralized authority structure represents a minimum loss of relevant autonomy for most institutions involved.

The emergency ambulance system and the referral transfers of patients between hospitals offer an interesting contrast.[10] In both cases the decisions to be made are highly routine and rely on simple rule systems. But in the case of referral transfers each hospital works out the arrangements for itself, while in the case of the emergency ambulance service a centralized authority structure is used. The source of this difference seems to lie in two interrelated factors: the number of cases handled and the urgency of the cases. The need to transfer patients occurs only occasionally and usually involves one or two cases. In contrast, each hospital linked to the ambulance service receives a dozen or more—sometimes many more—cases a day, and these must be handled as potential life-or-death emergencies. In short, the need for quick, coordinated action and the large number of cases processed require the near maximum use of both abstraction of rule systems and the inequality of centralized authority structures.

SOME COSTS OF CENTRALIZED AUTHORITY

Alternatives to centralized coordination may be unworkable for this particular function, but such centralization is not without its costs. The benefits from this type of centralization result in large measure from specifying and restricting channels of communication. But while such restrictions may increase the efficiency with which the typical case is handled (and therefore tend to improve the average level of efficiency), they may also decrease the efficiency for particular cases. When the cases fit the abstractions, efficiency is increased, but when they do not, problems arise. The ambulance system also illustrates this outcome. Our second observer reports:

One of the ambulance attendants . . . told me that he just spoke to a woman on the phone who wanted an ambulance. But she called Johnson directly, and he explained to her that she had to call [the central emergency number] because they were not allowed to go out on direct calls. . . . Just got the call in and it's [the same address] where the woman had called from originally. . . . It must have been a good twenty minutes from when they originally called. . . . it's just a block away from Johnson.

Clearly some cases do not conform to the abstract assumptions of the system, but the only response available is the standard one—even when it is inappropriate. Such undesirable outcomes point up one of the virtues of particularistic interaction: greater flexibility with respect to both available communication channels and possible responses.

The data indicate still another limitation of this centralized coordination. Concretely, this problem takes the form of faulty diagnoses of the need for an ambulance, and false alarm calls. Such calls represent, in theoretical terms, the inability of the authority structure to eliminate inappropriate or false communications. In part, this is a result of an open, virtually cost-free input system. Anyone who can make a phone call can request an ambulance. To a degree this would be true even if the system were not centralized. However, in a decentralized system ambulance crews are in close enough communication with those who accept calls so that phony requests would be more easily recognized and ignored or sanctioned. Centralized operators, in dealing with a larger population, have little chance of remembering the voice or the address of a repetitive abuser. Because centralized operators have very little if any direct communication with ambulance crews, there is little chance for meaningful feedback about inappropriate calls and thus little chance of reducing their number.

CONCLUSIONS

The data analysis in this chapter has several purposes. First, it illustrates in the context of interorganizational relations in the health system, the operation of one of the standard social mechanisms for improving the efficiency of coordinated decision making, that is, centralized authority structures. Second, it indicates the conditions under which such structures are likely to develop—even in institutional sectors where these mechanisms are not normally legitimate as a means of coordination. Third, it illustrates some of the limitations and weaknesses of these mechanisms in the context of urban health care systems.

But fourth and most important, the data analysis here serves to set the context for the next chapter. Centralized coordination by authority structures has been widely studied, and much of the discussion in this chapter has simply illustrated relatively well-known principles in the context of interorganizational relations between health care institutions. It was necessary, however, to introduce the information about this particular authority structure in order to be able to show how it is intimately related to other, less obvious mechanisms of interorganizational integration. We now turn to this task.

Chapter Four

THE QUASI-MARKET
IN PATIENT ALLOCATION

Markets purportedly address two interrelated problems. They make it easier for the individual to decide which combination of exchanges will best maximize that person's utility. On the collective level the market supposedly allocates resources and integrates activities so as to maximize production. To resolve either the individual or the collective problem by means of particularistic interaction would be extremely time consuming. In our terms markets simplify such decision-making through highly developed forms of abstraction. The most obvious example is through the standardization of weights, measures, and grades of commodities. But money prices are the case of abstraction par excellence; in principle the value of totally different items—tacks, turkeys, tanks, and TVs—can be expressed along the single common scale of dollars and cents. Therefore through money prices and standardized commodities we can quickly decide whether the best buy in butter is at store *A* or store *B*. The aggregate of such decisions determines how goods and services are allocated. By using the abstractions of the market—quantity, grade, and price—we greatly reduce the factors that must be taken into account and simplify the process of carrying out exchanges and allocating resources.

But the accuracy of these abstractions is based on the assumption that those who trade are roughly equal; for prices to reflect "true" value no buyer or seller must control enough of the commodity being traded to affect its price. Under such conditions goods and services are supposedly allocated in the most efficient possible manner. Therefore the abstraction and absence of inequality in the market supposedly interact to determine where goods and services are allocated: which consumers get how much butter, which factories get how much steel, which customers go to which barbershop.

A parallel question confronts our analysis of interorganizational relations on the Southside: which patients go to which institutions for treatment and why. But as we shall see, the abstractions of price and quality do not completely govern this allocation process. The "market" that allocates patients between institutions is highly imperfect; many of the assumptions of the classical conception of a market are violated. But this is true of many markets. The "market" that determines which brain surgeons are associated with which hospitals in Fairmont is probably as imperfect as the processes by which patients are allocated. Here is the key point: the mechanisms and procedures actually used to produce social integration are often considerably less neat than the ideal-typical models devised to describe these processes. Such models are, nevertheless, an essential beginning to fruitful analysis. We need, however, to press beyond these models and begin to specify concretely what structures create "imperfections" and to identify the hybrid, bastardized, and mixed types of social structures that have emerged. This chapter focuses on the role of the ambulance system and interorganizational inequality as factors that introduce imperfections into the allocation of patients; of equal concern will be why such imperfections are not erratic, unnecessary imperfections but are crucial to the current organization of health care.

THE ALLOCATION OF PATIENTS

The allocation of patients is a major aspect of the social order of a local health care system. What mechanisms prevent all the patients from going to a few hospitals while the other institutions remain empty? Or why do not all the obstetric cases end up in one hospital and all the heart attacks in another? What are the factors that determine who gets treated where? Of special interest is how this process produces the dual system of health care, that is, one set of institutions and services for poor people and another set for the more well-to-do.

The main regulators of the patient market are price differentials, geography, professional links, and religion. Although a few individuals may receive treatment completely free of charge, most are required to pay some portion if not all of the cost. (The services at Mercy cost more, even in the clinic, the wards, and the emergency room.) Such price differences encourage people with limited resources to go to less expensive institutions, even when the quality of care is lower. This is not a pure market situation regulated by prices. But it is a quasi-market and market prices are certainly not irrelevant.

Geography is another important determinant of patient allocation. The area around Mercy is predominantly middle class, while Johnson's neighborhood is overwhelmingly lower class. Nearly all of Johnson's patients who do not arrive by ambulance come from the surrounding lower class areas.

Two other factors tend to channel the more affluent patients toward Mercy: professional ties and religion. Nearly 60 percent of Mercy's private patients come from outside of the Southside and its adjoining regions. They come from all over the city and the suburbs. This results primarily from Mercy's good reputation among physicians in the metropolitan area. Perhaps personal ties among health professionals are even more important, for example, an internship or residency in past years or a medical school friend on the staff. Poor-quality hospitals like Johnson simply do not have this network of "assistants" who channel private patients to the institution. A second factor, religious affiliation, is important, though probably less so than in the past. Mercy has long-time ties with a particular religious denomination whose members are noted for their affluence and loyalty to denominational institutions. This contributes to Mercy's relative abundance of well-to-do patients.

THE LATENT FUNCTION OF THE AMBULANCE SERVICE

Money, geography, professional links, and religion are obviously important factors. A less obvious factor is nonetheless significant. The manifest purpose of the centralized ambulance service is to increase the efficiency of the entire health system by providing rapid transportation for the sick with a maximum of coordination and a minimum of duplication.

But at least within the Southside the organization of the ambulance service has an important latent function. It serves as a secondary regulator in the allocation of patients between hospitals. Just as geography and religion introduce "imperfections" into the market, the ambulance service is a key mechanism for biasing the outcome of the patient-allocation process.

Having the poorest hospital in the area operate the ambulance service results in the poorest and most ignorant patients' winding up at that hospital while the more affluent and knowledgeable are generally taken elsewhere. This is not to say ambulance crews or even the hospital admissions personnel screen patients explicitly in terms of social status. They do not need to, for low social status tends to be correlated with ignorance, passivity, and disabling forms of illness. Patients are taken to Johnson unless they specifically request not to be taken there. It is the more knowledgeable who take the necessary action to avoid Johnson. But sometimes knowledge is not enough. One observer mentioned a young boy who was not asked where he wanted to go. The second observer comments on the case of the nine-year-old child who was taken to Johnson despite his vociferous protest.

It seems a minor has no rights. . . . He gets taken to Johnson unless his mother signs a request for him to go to another hospital. Since the child's mother wasn't there they took him to Johnson. They had to wait for the mother to give permission to give treatment, but you don't need permission to be taken in an ambulance.

Another aspect of patient allocation under the influence of the ambulance service concerns patients with chronic crises or problems. Our second observer describes some specific instances:

We're on the corner of Alexander and 5th Street, and there is a fellow lying passed out. Looks like he's having an epileptic fit; he's drooling from the mouth; his legs are out straight. . . . They're taking him now and putting him in the ambulance. I just found out from the ambulance attendant that the fellow we just picked up now . . . was picked up about 2:00 [an hour and a half before], and brought to Johnson. It seems he just walked out of the building. . . . He has the DT's from drinking. . . . Doctor on duty said he didn't leave more than ten or fifteen minutes ago. The ambulance driver—without even having to look up a record—was able to put down the patient's name and address. The ambulance attendant told me he's brought in here at least a couple of times a week . . .

sometimes two or three times a day. He's an alcoholic and there just isn't anything they can do about it.

I was talking to one of the drivers about how often this happens. . . . He was talking about one lady whom he called a hypochondriac who calls about three times every 24 hours—once for each of the 8-hour shifts. She happens to be an outpatient over at Mercy's OPD [Outpatient Department]. They told them not even to bring her by anymore; they don't even want to take her in.

Apparently in the past the sorting was done much more explicitly. According to Mr. Kaufmann, director of CAS, municipal hospitals formerly had to accept all cases sent to them by other hospitals:

This meant that any hospital in the city, if for any reason they didn't want this particular case, could send him to Wattsbury or some other municipal hospital. . . . The result was a lot of abuses, and this came out rather strongly in the State investigation. . . . A lot of dumping was going on: meaning that a hospital would get a case and say we don't want this case—for whatever reason, uninteresting medically, doesn't have the money to pay—they would . . . dispatch the patient out to another hospital. This has been cut back a bit. . . .

Mercy's administrator, Michael George, was quite adamant that his hospital does not engage in "dumping."

The only agreement we have in the transfer of acute patients is when a patient may come into our emergency room and we don't have any beds. We've lowered our average length of stay, but still find that we're filled to capacity day in and day out. I get across my desk every morning a copy of the patients we've transferred the night before, just to make sure that these patients were in need of acute care and we did not have a bed.

Residents in charge of admissions in medicine and in surgery, questioned about this point, said patients were transferred only in the rare instances when literally no beds were available. If Mercy ever engaged in extensive "dumping" it apparently has been eliminated or significantly reduced.

In summary the main mechanism for sorting patients via the ambulance service is not the deliberate transfer of unwanted cases. Rather the ambulance service is organized so that the poor, the ignorant, the young, and the acutely and chronically sick are the least likely to overcome the organizational procedures that channel them toward Johnson.

But now we need to consider why Johnson performs a service that tends to channel the "good" patients to other institutions and leave them with the "dregs."

SCRAPS FROM THE TABLE

Johnson continues the service because, despite the fact that a high percentage of those picked up do not come to Johnson, a significant portion of the *paying* patients that do come to Johnson arrive via the ambulance service. These are usually the patients with some type of health insurance. Approximately 75 percent of the hospital's inpatients are admitted through the emergency room; roughly half of these arrive in the ambulance. Moreover, those arriving by ambulance often require extensive treatment and therefore have higher bills. Exactly how much income is provided by the patients arriving by ambulance is unclear. In view of the hospital's extremely critical financial condition, this income is essential to the institution's survival.

Johnson may also operate the ambulance service because they "make money" on their contract with the city. The Johnson administration claims the ambulance operation costs more than they receive from the city in reimbursement. As we shall see, when Mercy was considering the possibility of operating an ambulance (under a more or less identical contract with the city) they estimated that "you could make a little, but not much." Therefore Johnson may get another scrap by making a little "profit" off the ambulance contract. The bigger of the two scraps is, however, almost certainly the increase in paying patients that the ambulance service produces.

READJUSTMENT OF THE SORTING SYSTEM

The weakening of the class screening and matching functions of the ambulance service has been accompanied by a change in Mercy's attitude toward this service. For a number of years Mercy steadfastly refused to operate an ambulance service. In the last five years this policy position has been completely reversed. Mercy now wants to operate an ambulance service, and the city has approved this change in principle. However, the proposed service has never actually been put into operation.

Mercy's changed attitude and policy is probably related to the changed legal requirements regarding nonpaying patients. Hospitals must treat all patients who come to their emergency room. The avoidance of an ambulance service no longer enables a hospital to avoid nonpaying emergency patients.[1]

In addition, pressure to operate an ambulance purportedly came from community groups. Michael George, the administrator of Mercy stated:

> Our community just could not understand how they could put in a call for an ambulance and have the ambulance from Johnson Hospital ride right by Mercy down to 40th Street, pick up a patient and ride right by the emergency room at Mercy Hospital when, in fact, this patient may have been a known patient at Mercy Hospital for 20 years.

But later the associate administrator with special responsibility for these matters, Fred Zarati, was asked to specify the nature of the community pressure:

*I:** Who do you mean by the "community?"

R: Well, I don't know who I mean by the "community."

I: Where have you heard this?

R: O.K. . . . It goes back a long time. One of the original councils that we had working with the hospital was the Southside Health Committee, the advisory group to the Heightsville Community Health Center (HCHC). They were one of the early groups that asked that Mercy Hospital have an ambulance.

I: How long ago was that?

R: I guess about three or four years ago. The Urban Health Advisory Council, which . . . is really an advisory committee to our outpatient department, has asked the institution to look into an ambulance service. It is hard to remember, but it was various community groups of some sort that have asked the institution to look into an ambulance service.

Considering that on other issues community groups have subjected Mercy to public protest, picketing, and even sit-ins, this vaguely defined community pressure is unlikely to be the sole or even the primary source of the changed attitude toward operating ambulances. It has, however, been a contributing factor.

The support for an ambulance service by the hospital's surgeons is

I stands for interviewer; *R* stands for respondent.

probably another factor in the change of attitude and policy. When asked the reason for this change by our interviewer, the head of the department of surgery replied:

I'm not really sure. I don't know the thinking involved when there was opposition to it, but from my own point of view, and that of the surgical service, it's a good thing to have an ambulance. I'm looking forward to it; I think it will increase our opportunities to take care of . . . you know . . . acute problems, surgical problems.

In contrast the department of medicine is considerably less enthusiastic. For them the ambulance poses the possibility of a high percentage of "uninteresting" cases and "disposition problems": mainly cases for which the diagnosis is obvious, patients for whom the possibility of effective treatment is limited, and patients who might tie up scarce beds for extended periods (for example, old people with strokes).

As far as could be determined no open power struggle between the surgical and medical departments developed over this issue, possibly because the medical department felt that they were bound to lose. Quite likely this change in the relative importance of having an adequate number of trauma cases[2] for teaching purposes is related to the hospital's recent, more intense affiliation with a medical school. If this is so, one type of interorganizational relationship, the teaching affiliation, has produced a shift in the relative influence of the two most important departments in Mercy, at least with respect to this issue. This in turn is going to change the nature of a second set of interorganizational relationships, the neighborhood ambulance service.

So far we have considered three factors that may have contributed to Mercy's changed policy toward an ambulance service: new rules and pressure requiring that all patients who come to the emergency room be treated, whether or not they are able to pay; explicit though limited pressure from community organizations; and pressure from the surgical department, which may in turn be related to the new medical school affiliation. There are additional factors. First is the position of the City Ambulance Service (CAS). Johnson Hospital is located almost at one end of a long, narrow ambulance district. Consequently, a long time is required for the ambulance to respond to a call from the other end of the district and return to the Johnson emergency room. CAS, understandably wishes to locate the ambulances nearer the center of the district. Mercy is more centrally located, and therefore creating an ambulance service there fits in with the CAS desires and policy.

COMPLEXITY AND DELAY: NEUTRALIZATION

Yet, even with this convergence of interest among the more powerful participants, those involved were not able to reach even a policy decision giving Mercy an ambulance service, much less implement the change. There were objections. If Mercy, the city, and community groups are for it, who can stand against it? Surprisingly enough, Johnson Hospital. Ironically, Johnson was able to do so precisely because its financial condition was so critical. The Johnson administration argued that, if the neighborhood ambulance service were taken away from them, the significant reduction in their number of paying patients would force them out of business. Quite likely both the city and Mercy would have some qualms about triggering such an event on purely moral and altruistic grounds. Clearly the neighborhood needs more health care facilities, not fewer. But Mercy also had a significant self-interest in avoiding the collapse of Johnson. The administrator of Mercy explained the problem this way:

They [Johnson] have a clinic [outpatient department] population of about 100,000 people. Many of their paying patients were brought into the hospital as a result of the ambulances. We were quite concerned that if we took their ambulance district away from them, this would stop the influx of inpatients and cause them to go right out of business—and what in God's name would we do with another 100,000 outpatients coming to our outpatient clinics! We see over 240,000 outpatients now.

Obviously this realization placed Mercy in a real dilemma. They wanted an ambulance service, but they did not want an extra 100,000 low-income outpatients.

The solution was in principle relatively simple. The city simply redrew the prospective ambulance district boundaries so that both Johnson and Mercy have a district. It is generally conceded that Mercy got the "better part" of the old district, the part with more middle- and upper-income residents. However, it is hoped that the proposed new district for Johnson will provide enough patients to keep them afloat.

Still Mercy has no ambulance service, despite an increasingly long-standing agreement in principle. Several factors have prevented its introduction. One complication is the administrative setup that Mercy tentatively worked out. Unlike the Johnson arrangement, Mercy would prefer not to own and operate the ambulances themselves. They want access to the ambulance cases but do not want the service identified with the hospital. After much consideration the city agreed to maintain ownership and operation of an ambulance service based at Mercy.

There were, however, at least two factors favoring Mercy's operating the ambulances directly. One was money. Harry Smith, the assistant to the executive director, claimed that with a reimbursement from the city of $80,000 per ambulance per year, "if you run it well you can make a little money—not a lot, but you can more than break even." A second consideration may have been Mercy's ability to influence the actions of the ambulance crews who are their own employees. Apparently this is particularly important with respect to which types of patients would be brought back to Mercy and which ones would be taken to other hospitals. Harry Smith said:

From what I understand, you can have fairly good control over your drivers, if you desire to. . . . You could simply instruct your drivers: uninteresting cases or cases that will ultimately be disposition problems should be taken elsewhere, and bring us only interesting cases.

Whatever the factors that made Mercy's decision difficult, they finally concluded that they would prefer for the city to have direct operational responsibilities. Given the fact that Mercy would probably be able to maintain adequate control over the ambulance crews, any small "profit" they might make seemed to be offset by what Harry Smith described as "union considerations, and all the other problems that go along with having another group of specialized employees, and also lack of physical space to handle these people."

But the decision to "let the city do it" actually led to much of the delay in the initiation of the service, because the CAS was unable to locate a suitable place to house the ambulances and staff. In addition, internal problems at Mercy also contributed to the delay. To handle the new load the ambulance service would bring, Mercy felt they must do two things: set up a special emergency room for pediatric cases and install x-ray equipment in the old emergency room. Financing and construction problems delayed the accomplishment of these projects and hence the initiation of the ambulance service.

We see how many complex factors enter into attempts to change interorganizational relations. The interest and limitations of so many actors must be taken into account that it has been impossible to implement a decision even after approval in principle by all the relevant parties. Attempts to increase efficiency by raising the level of coordination have ironically had the opposite effect. The greater complexity and delays have, in addition, increased the time and cost and decreased the probability of implementing this change.

THE TWO FACES OF INTEGRATION AND CHANGE

The proposed change in the neighborhood ambulance service is like a person's reflection in a fun house. What you look like depends on which mirror you look in. One mirror reflects a picture of increased integration, efficiency, and equality. The other reflection shows the same old status quo. Who really benefits from the higher level of interorganizational integration that would supposedly result from the proposed arrangements? Is it primarily the neighborhood health care system and the patients it serves that will gain? Or will the benefits go mainly to Mercy hospital?

Clearly, locating an ambulance station in the center of the district rather than at one end makes good sense. Undoubtedly patients in the vicinity of Mercy who have an ongoing relationship with that institution should be taken there rather than somewhere else. Certainly the surgery department at a teaching hospital should be ensured a sufficient number of trauma cases. These changes must be especially worthwhile if they can be made without seriously jeopardizing Johnson's critical financial condition.

But there is another picture too, that of a dominant institution increasing its control over one of the important sorting mechanisms in the neighborhood health system. The old mechanisms—refusing all but limited treatment to those who cannot pay and "dumping" via transfers to other hospitals—are no longer allowed, and new mechanisms must be developed. Mercy may not ever have to use the new mechanism—pressure the ambulance crews to take unwanted patients elsewhere—because the proportion of "good" to "bad" patients may remain satisfactory, or at least tolerable, because of other factors such as geographical location. But they will at least have the possibility at their disposal.

So both images seem to be real. The proposed change may improve the health care in the neighborhood, though all admit that the improvement would be only marginal. But at the same time, the quality, status, and power of Mercy are likely to improve. The neighborhood will more than likely continue to have both a "shithouse" and a "glamour joint."

Chapter Five

PARTICULARISTIC INTERACTION

As we have seen, the usual mechanisms of simplification and integration—centralized authority and competitive markets—are rarely used in the health sector to regulate interorganizational relationships. When they are present they tend to be highly "imperfect." Consequently, mutual adjustment through particularistic interaction is common. That is, organizations in the health and welfare sector tend to integrate their activities by developing sets of mutual expectations. They do this through sequences of interaction between specific organizations. In this chapter we look at (1) some of the interorganizational links developed by this means and (2) some of the factors that encourage or retard the development of such particularistic relationships. As might be anticipated from the earlier discussion we examine the role of organizational inequality in the formation of these relationships. The chapter also considers how simple universalistic rules serve as a substitute for particularistic relationships when the content of the interorganizational link deals with highly standardized routine issues.

THE FARMING-OUT SYSTEM

Much of Johnson Hospital's deterioration is due to a failure to move ahead rather than to an absolute decline. Dr. Steuben, Chief of Medicine at Johnson, comments on this issue:

It isn't that we farm out things that used to be done here. We must farm out things that should now be done here. We are practicing medicine roughly as it was practiced following the second World War or around the period of the second World War . . . Since that time fantastic explosions have occurred—not only in buildings, but in medicine, and Johnson has not been exploding with it.

The primary way that Johnson has managed not to be overcome by this explosion is by an extensive "farming-out" operation. That is, needed services are secured from or referred to other institutions. These outside services are secured in four different ways.

Referrals and Transfers

Johnson has no dental facilities. A simple referral and transfer is made for dental services, as described by Dr. Juan Martinez, Director of Ambulatory Care:

We are doing all our dental work at Wattsbury Hospital. In other words if a patient in the hospital has a toothache, I automatically put him through Wattsbury . . . we send the patient over there; when they finish . . . they send him back.

This type of cooperation involves a formal (in the sense of impersonal) but noncontractual relationship between two institutions. Wattsbury is a city hospital required to treat patients sent to them. This procedure is not due to any unique personal particularistic relationships between members of the staff. Rather it results from the formal rules of the city's health system. This same relationship would exist no matter who was director of ambulatory care. As we shall see, this is not true of many of the farming-out linkages.

Psychiatric and obstetric care are other areas where Johnson must in large part rely on impersonal referrals to other institutions. Part-time psychiatrists on the staff deal with ambulatory patients in the emergency room. However, someone needing inpatient care must be sent to another institution. The major city hospitals do have psychiatric wards, and patients are normally transferred to one of these institutions, depending on their place of residence. Obstetric cases are handled in a similar manner; they are referred or transferred to the city hospital closest to the patient's place of residence. Obstetric services were discontinued at Johnson about fifteen years ago; in this respect Johnson has not only failed to keep up, but has regressed.

The city hospitals to which referrals are made definitely rank in the lower end of the dual system, though their facilities and status are significantly better than Johnson's. While to some extent the assistance of city hospitals is due to legal requirements, this does not explain the full extent of their cooperation. If legal requirements were the only factor involved, the help they give Johnson might be considerably more niggardly. The referral and transfer process in fact operates in both directions, but it is undoubtedly more essential to Johnson than to the other hospitals. City-operated hospitals make transfers to Johnson when they have no empty beds. According to Dr. Martinez, transfers to Mercy and other high-status institutions seldom occur by this means—though as we shall see they come about for other reasons. By participating in this city-wide exchange system among the have-not hospitals, Johnson obtains not only beds during peak periods and extra inpatients during slow periods but also important special services such as dentistry, obstetrics, and psychiatric care.

Transfers via Physicians with Dual Appointments

But referrals and transfers to the better-off low-status institutions are not the only way that Johnson secures vital services. A second means is through part-time specialists whose primary appointment is with a high-status institution. Neurosurgery and cardiology are handled in this fashion. According to Dr. Martinez, "The cardiology is done at Mellon [Mellon Medical School-City General Hospital] because the cardiologist, Dr. Jacques, works both here and at Mellon. When we need a cardiac catheterization he arranges it . . . he takes the patient to Mellon."

The neurosurgeon, Dr. William Flacks, is on the staff of Mercy. He screens patients suspected of having neurological problems requiring surgery. Dr. Martinez described this working procedure:

. . . no [neurological] patient goes through here without Flacks having looked at the patient. In this way we solve the problem that the attending physician thought that a test [at Mercy] was necessary and when the patient arrives there the neurosurgeon does not feel the test is necessary.

This screening is done because Mercy and particularly Dr. Flacks do not consider the Johnson staff qualified to handle such matters. It was not possible to record the interview with Dr. Flacks, but the interviewer's field notes are instructive about the nature of the Flacks–Johnson relationship.

Dr. Flacks has practiced from Johnson for ten years. He very strongly denounced the operation of the hospital. Some of his verbatim comments were "It should be closed." "At best it is only marginal." "The diagnostic facilities are nonexistent for my kind of work." When asked about . . . transferring patients from Johnson to Mercy, he said that if the patient had insurance there was no problem. If the patient poses no financial burden on Mercy then he was transferred. In the case of ward patients who need diagnostic studies, the arrangements are made on the "administrative level." "Normally, the ward patients spend only one day undergoing tests, [and] the patient is not boarded at Mercy. In the cases where . . . special studies have to be made, e.g., special diagnostic x-ray procedures, the patient is kept at Mercy 24 to 48 hours . . . if the patient he has examined needs surgery, and if he is insured . . . he is transferred to Mercy . . . as Dr. Flack's private patient. If he is uninsured . . . he is admitted to the ward. He spent a great deal of time explaining the inadequacy of Johnson and the fact that he could in no way use Johnson facilities without leaving himself open to malpractice suits. . . . He again stressed the fact that the staff was not qualified. He was asked why, with his aversion to Johnson, he was still affiliated with it after ten years. He was quite frank and said that a goodly portion of his patient load came from Johnson. In other words, he was making money.

In contrast to the referral and transfer for dentistry, psychiatry, and obstetrics—which are impersonal relationships—the linkages in cardiology and neurosurgery are based on key staff members' holding dual appointments. Patients transferred under this arrangement are not received as "Johnson patients" but as "a patient of Dr. Flacks."

It is apparent how both Johnson and the individual doctors benefit from this arrangement. What may be less obvious is how the high-status hospitals benefit. Even large teaching hospitals like Mercy do not have enough patients to justify highly developed specialized services in all areas of medical care. This is the case with neurosurgery. But small, less developed, and less prestigious departments like neurosurgery are an important institutional asset; they provide consultations and help the hospital maintain a full array of services. Mercy probably could not afford to have such specialists on their staff if they did not have links to poor-quality hospitals. Dual appointments at two high-status institutions would not produce the same result. Such an appointment might give the doctor enough private patients to provide him an "adequate" income and consequently spread the cost of this high-priced personnel among several institutions. But providing specialized services such as neurosurgery involves fixed costs for the hospital in equipment and overhead. These costs are kept tolerable only if there are a sufficient number of patients utilizing the special service. The number of patients treated at a given high-status hospital is increased only by such specialists having links to low-status institutions that make no attempt to provide this service.

The Gracious-Colleague Arrangement

A third type of farming-out linkage, like the second, is based on personal, particularistic relationships. In the case of cardiology and neurosurgery, the specialist's primary appointment is at the high-status institution, with secondary relationships to Johnson. In pathology, the opposite is true; the specialist's primary appointment is at Johnson.

Dr. Ravel, the chief of pathology, tells how he happened to come to Johnson and describes the problems he faces:

R: I came here to work in gynecologic pathology . . . the chief here was Dr. Snowman. He is a very well-known specialist in gynecologic pathology. Six months later he resigned.

I: And you moved into the directorship?

R: Yes. That was not my dream!

I: It's a difficult situation?

R: Very, very difficult, very. The frustrations that you have here . . . Only if you work here . . . can you understand! No money to pay for products that I need for everyday tests. The companies call and they say, "We cannot deliver because your hospital owes us $1,000." And . . . you will see where the girls [technicians] are working . . . and where they do the urinalysis. You would never dream in this country you would see something like that!

That the facilities are inadequate is hardly surprising. What is surprising, however, are Dr. Ravel's professional reputation and contacts. The majority of the physicians at Johnson do not conduct research and do not have appointments at high-status institutions. In contrast Dr. Ravel is on the faculty of University Medical School and was formerly connected with a reputable, if not prestigious, research-oriented hospital. His department at Johnson's is accredited to train residents in pathology—though for only the first two years of what is normally a four-year program. He readily admits that the resident program is weak, in large measure because of the cases available for teaching material. Since few people have elective surgery at Johnson, the residents tend to see only the types of problems that occur in emergency rooms.

Dr. Ravel extends the facilities available for both hospital testing and training by using personal contacts he has outside Johnson. To a significant degree he is successful in broadening the type of cases his residents see by arranging for them to attend seminars and conferences at other institutions. However, this does not solve the basic problem; they do not get the experience of routinely conducting all the various tests, because the necessary equipment and supplies are not available. Dr. Ann Smithfield, another pathologist, works part time at both Johnson and Fairfield. Through her the Fairfield laboratory can be used for tests, but this is seldom much help, since it is little better than the Johnson laboratory.

To overcome some of the problems, Dr. Ravel tried at one point to transform his personal link with the University Medical School into an interorganizational link between the University and Johnson.

R: Now I wanted very much to have an affiliation with the [University Medical School] department. I even went to Dr. Ross [chief of pathology at the University] and said, "Look, I will give you [the University] my salary [at Johnson]. You can send people to us and I will send people to you. Our hospital will still pay the residents." He thought for a while and said, "Well, I'm very glad you are appointed here; you can come to the conferences and you can send your residents. But in any stronger affiliation we would not be interested."

The appointment at the University is very good. You can use the library; you can go to all the meetings; and you can use the club; they are very nice about it.

I: But not . . . their lab? [That is, use it for the routine tests needed for Johnson patients.]

R: Oh, no! . . . I don't really understand . . . I think that a medical school like University should take care of the small hospitals.

Up to this point we have dealt with farming-out mechanisms involving little or no cash outlay for Johnson. Dental, psychiatric, and obstetric needs are met by sending patients to public institutions required to accept such cases. Cardiology and neurosurgery are handled by specialists who have a secondary relationship with Johnson and primary appointments at high-status hospitals that can provide these services. Pathology is kept afloat by the ability of the relatively high-status chief of the department to "beg and borrow" from friends and colleagues at other institutions. But there are limits to what even the most ingenious staff can do without money, and some services simply have to be purchased—the fourth farming-out technique.

The Purchase of Services

Most of the purchases involve radioactive procedures at Mercy, especially "scanning." This technique is central to much diagnostic work.

When a Johnson physician decides that a procedure at Mercy is required, he notifies Martinez. Martinez has his assistant make an appointment with the appropriate office at Mercy. Then he calls the Johnson ambulance office and arranges for transportation to Mercy. The medical procedure is then performed by the Mercy staff, and Johnson is billed. If they find anything abnormal—a tumor is discovered, for example—the results are usually phoned to Martinez, and a full report is sent back with the patient's chart. When nothing is wrong the report is sent by mail. If the patient is all right and ready for release, he is released directly from Mercy. When an operation is required that can be performed at Johnson, he is returned via the ambulance.

Martinez seems to be quite satisfied with this arrangement.

I: How do you feel about working with Mercy? Are they fairly cooperative with you?

R: From my point of view I have a beautiful relationship with them. I never really run into the slightest argument. . . . One day I visited them to find out exactly to whom I was talking by phone. . . . Today [now] automatically the doctor sees the scanning over there. If there is anything abnormal, they automatically call me. . . . That is more than a favor.

This purchase of services from Mercy is a significant help in keeping Johnson from being even further behind the times. Moreover, Johnson can thereby keep the paying inpatients who would otherwise have to be transferred to other hospitals. In such cases the fees paid to Mercy for the scanning are relatively insignificant compared to the total income Johnson gains by being able to keep (rather than transfer) the patient.

Of course, Mercy undoubtedly gains from the arrangement too. The radioactive procedures require very expensive equipment and a minimum number of highly paid staff even if they are not heavily used.

Because Mercy equipment is not utilized to maximum capacity, servicing Johnson's patients helps cut costs.

An interesting footnote on the Johnson–Mercy relationship concerns the way the scanning arrangements were initiated. Mr. Zarati, one of the associate administrators at Mercy, tells the story:

> The way it actually started was that we had a monstrous machine called the whole body counter . . . a research type machine . . . you actually enter it like a submarine. It's counting things like potassium levels, the water in the body. . . . What they were trying to show was that if there was any fluctuation that was other than normal it would indicate some sort of disease. . . . In order to establish what was normal and what was not normal . . . we had, I think every child in the neighborhood schools in here. We had all the patients, all the staff of the hospital—to provide different levels of normalcy. And also a lot of Johnson patients. We went to Johnson . . . and they said, "Sure," and that started the relationships. . . . Then Dr. Martinez came and said maybe we can do other things. . . . He came to see me . . . and also . . . one of the assistant directors in the department of medicine. . . . It just started building that way.

Mercy has unquestionably been genuinely cooperative and helpful to Johnson in a way that cannot be accounted for simply by any short-term financial gain. Nonetheless one wonders whether the response to Dr. Martinez would have been as cordial if Johnson had not at an earlier time been a helpful supplier of the "whole bodies."

Conclusion

The theme of this section is a simple one: marginal institutions like Johnson manage to function and survive in large measure because of a wide array of linkages with other health care institutions. Some of these linkages are with high-status institutions such as Mercy. Some are with other institutions that, like Johnson, "specialize" in treating the poor but are larger and have a greater array of facilities. Of course all organizations have linkages to their environment whereby they secure vital resources. But it is unusual for these resources to come from organizations of the same general type. Ford Motor Company is highly dependent on U.S. Steel and the United Automobile Workers, but they do not receive major resources or services from General Motors. The Red Cross may cooperate with the Salvation Army, but they keep their dependency on the latter very limited. The difference is that Johnson is highly dependent on the cooperation and help of other health facilities to carry out the minimal routine activities normally associated with an urban hospital. Consequently, Johnson is extremely vulnerable to the actions of the other health care institutions to which it is linked. Why are these outside agents so helpful when the interdependence often seems to be so asymmetrical? We return to this question at the end of the chapter.

The Ambulance Service and the Farming-Out System

The material in the preceding sections implicitly indicates the importance of the ambulance service for the farming-out system. Officially ambulances should not be used for the routine transfer of patients.[1] But Johnson squeezes these transfers in between emergency calls. This means that patients scheduled for tests at Mercy may be delayed because of emergency calls. In fact when the transfer arrangement was first initiated Mercy frequently complained about this. Dr. Martinez solved this problem by placing a "fake time" on the form he sends to the ambulance drivers requesting a transfer. "They give me an appointment at Mercy for 10:00; I put . . . 9:30. That way if the ambulance is delayed, the patient will arrive on time." We see, in this context, another important benefit that Johnson derives in operating the ambulance service. The farming-out system would simply not be practical if Johnson did not have ambulances directly under their control.

There is one final point of interest. The social mechanism developed to cope with conflicting demands on the ambulances is the "fake time." It is the lubricant that allows the gears of interorganizational relations to mesh rather than grind. But we should not overlook the source from which this lubricant is extracted: increased waiting time for lower class patients and more work for the ambulance crews. In view of Johnson's overall problems and needs, this is probably a small cost to pay; who pays the cost is both unsurprising and instructive.

COOPERATION AMONG THE HAVE-NOTS·

Intermittently since the beginning of recorded time reformers and radicals have exhorted peasants to organize themselves for mutual betterment. Sometimes the vision has been of the disadvantaged "pulling themselves up by their bootstraps" through peaceful hard work. At other times the emphasis has been on the overthrow of some exploiting group. Although major transformations occasionally result, attempts to organize a revolution of the disadvantaged—whether peaceful or violent—have not been noted for their high rate of success. In some cases the exhortation falls on deaf ears, in others there is much talk and little else, in others peaceful hard work produces few significant gains, and in still others heroic revolutionary actions are brutally repressed.

In the Southside neighborhood the peasants of the health system are for the most part in the talking stage. While there is plenty of hostility toward the privileged—high-status health institutions and physicians, as well as middle- and upper-class patients—most of the talk is about cooperation and coordination rather than revolution. Yet relatively few working cooperative relationships between have-not institutions are of major significance to either the overall health care in the neighborhood or the institutions involved. In this section we shall do three things: look at some of the rhetoric about cooperation, examine a case or two where actions contradict this rhetoric, and examine one critical instance where close day-to-day cooperation between two institutions in fact occurs.

Rhetoric and Reality

Typically ideologies include sets of highly idealized norms and exaggerate the degree of conformity to these norms. Moreover the degree of verbal conformity is usually considerably higher than behavioral conformity. This phenomenon is well illustrated in the Southside's health institutions.

Johnson and Bernstein are a quarter to a third of a mile apart. No major physical or ecological barriers separate them. They are similar, especially with respect to the problems and difficulties they face. Long-range plans call for a merger of the two hospitals and the construction of a "health park," but this will probably not happen in less than ten years—possibly much longer. Despite much talk about cooperation and coordination, over a two- or three-year period relatively little seems to have actually happened. Mrs. Helen Walker, administrator of Johnson:

One of the things that the community is trying to develop is this Wattsbury Coalition for Health Care . . . which would be an overall cooperative venture by most of the health institutions in the area. . . . So that we conceive our future role as being an alliance with various other institutions that service the neighborhood community. We also hope that there will be a much closer relationship between Johnson Hospital and Bernstein which is down the street here. . . . All of these things are in the process of being developed at this time.

About the same time this interview took place Dr. Ravel became the chief pathologist. He tells about his attempt to develop cooperative relationships with Bernstein:

I tried. I called the pathologist there. "Look, I just took the job as director of the laboratory at Johnson; how about trying to work out some programs together?" He doesn't have an approved residents' program and I have. He said, "Well, I don't need you." I said, "Yes, I know you don't need me, but maybe we can work something together." I tried to be very nice to him. Finally I convinced him that maybe we could get together for lunch, but he never called me.

Mrs. Sarah Jones, director of social services at Johnson, comments on the relationship with other institutions:

As far as other hospitals are concerned, unfortunately there's very little communication except on a transfer basis. There should be more now. . . . I've just started that with Bernstein for the first time.

She explains that this initial contact with Bernstein centers on a new proposed drug addiction program, which was mentioned by a number of respondents as an example of a cooperative program between Johnson and Bernstein. The plan called for Johnson to have ten to fifteen beds for drug detoxification of men, while Bernstein was to have a slightly fewer number for women. The rationale for this division of labor was that Bernstein has an obstetric service, which is required for women patients since many of them are pregnant. Supposedly neither hospital had sufficient room or facilities for both men and women. More than two years after the initial conversation with Mrs. Jones, the program was still not off the ground and had been virtually abandoned. The funding agency was blamed for the delay. Although informal communication between the social service departments may have improved, no formal tie had been developed.

Cooperation by Intrapersonal Linkages

In one area of medical services, pediatrics, Johnson and Bernstein are closely linked; Dr. Horace Mooreman, an extraordinary person, is director of pediatrics at both hospitals. He has appointments at four hospitals, Johnson, Bernstein, Mercy, and Baptist General. That he has admitting privileges at the latter two speaks well for his professional reputation. In addition he is on the faculty of University Medical School as an associate in pediatrics, participates in a prepaid group practice, is in effect the medical director for a children's foster care agency, presides over the medical board at Johnson, and sits on the board of a medical research foundation. His multitude of activities and positions make him a walking interorganizational network. His numerous appointments facilitate the transfer of pediatric patients between hospitals whenever the need for additional services or space is apparent. Yet, interorganizational cooperation exists only in matters that are under Dr. Mooreman's total control and authority. Other areas of pediatrics are not generally coordinated or integrated between organizations.

Perhaps even the pediatrics linkage is not an example of formal interorganizational cooperation. Rather the relationship seems to be due almost entirely to Dr. Mooreman's unique dual role. Of course if there were a definite commitment from two hospitals to have a common director of pediatrics this would be a form of official organizational cooperation. This does not seem to be the case, for it is by no means apparent that if Dr. Mooreman resigned another joint appointment would be made. Dr. Mooreman's own appointment was not a joint action per se; rather, he was known at Bernstein and available and was asked to fill in when a vacancy suddenly occurred. The majority of interorganizational linkages—both those between hospitals of the same status and links between low- and high-status institutions—seem to be based on personal rather than either organizational or geographical factors. Dr. Mooreman describes the difficulties:

R: The neurologist there [Marconi Hospital]—again it's a completely personal relationship—is an excellent lady. She and I interned together. I can call her up and say, "I've got such and such a case. . . ." But anybody who doesn't have a tie like that, God help them. If I have a child who's placed out in Highland Park. . . . You know sometimes it can take half a day just to find out who the doctor is much less anything else. There is no mechanism to do this unless you know the person, or unless you can take the time and get somebody's sympathy. I think the biggest problem is communication.

I: Do you have this problem with hospitals that are close geographically, or is it serious anywhere?

R: I don't think the closeness makes as much difference as having some contacts—or at least knowing the set-up even if you don't know anybody anymore; if you know how things are run in that hospital you know who to ask for.

I: Have there been any real efforts made to overcome that?

R: Not that I know of.

Inequality and Interorganizational Links

One of the key findings is that few cooperative relationships develop between low-status organizations, but many develop between low-status and high-status institutions. The consequences of inequality for integration can be roughly divided into two dimensions: differentiation of function and differentiation of power, influence, and status. Frequently inequality means that different actors not only have different levels of resources but that they also perform different activities within the larger collectivity. Johnson "specializes" in giving minimum levels of care to poor patients with common types of illness. Mercy, on the other hand, serves a much larger proportion of upper- and middle-class patients. Partly as a corollary of this they have the staff and facilities to treat more unusual, esoteric ailments. The interorganizational inequality means that to a significant degree the two hospitals do different things. This provides a basis for complementarity and therefore cooperation.

When we look at the relationships between Johnson and higher status hospitals these considerations definitely come into play. Higher status institutions obviously have resources of value to the lower status institution. Yet this does not account for all the cooperative links unless we are willing to assume that the well-to-do institutions are engaged in altruistic charity to their less fortunate cousins. One asset the lower status institutions provide is patients with unusual illnesses. The more esoteric the service or technology, the smaller the proportion of the population requiring such facilities, and therefore the larger the population pool must be to justify the existence of such facilities. Consequently hospitals like Mercy require links to institutions that have the potential for initially identifying esoteric needs but not the capacity for treating them. The result is the channeling of additional patients from low-status to high-status hospitals. Usually this tends to take the form of referrals, but in special cases such as the Johnson–Mercy relationship, the high-status institution performs the service while the clients continue to be patients at the low-status institution. This latter arrangement gives the high-status institution additional and needed esoteric cases while it allows the lower status one to provide—and charge for—all the services it is capable of offering.

A second kind of differentiation is probably more important; as indicated, the low-status institutions "specialize" almost entirely in lower class patients. Such patients have special medical problems that are difficult and expensive to treat, for example, drug addiction. Or alternatively they have very common ailments (which are therefore not medically interesting)—for example, strokes in older people. If lower status institutions did not exist in the same geographical area as the high-status ones, the latter would have to treat even larger numbers of these "undesirable" cases. We return to this theme later, but the important point is that organizational inequality among hospitals produces various types of differentiation so that it is to the advantage of *both* the low-status and high-status institutions to enter into various kinds of cooperative relationships.

When we look at low-status hospitals, these same factors help us understand the absence of linkages. There is very little worth sharing or exchanging. As Dr. Ravel (Johnson's director of pathology) indicated, he can send specimens to Fairfield Hospital for tests, but this is little help, since their laboratory is no better than Johnson's. In principle Dr. Mooreman could further integrate the pediatrics departments of Johnson and Bernstein by developing different types of specialization at each hospital. But even with a combined department, they cannot afford or justify the specialty services they now secure from the higher status hospitals. Each hospital must have a minimum level of equipment and staff to have a pediatrics service, but when this minimum is about all that each institution has, there is nothing to share.

However, when hospitals are filled to capacity, the opposite pattern emerges in the transfer of patients. Transfers are usually made to hospitals of approximately the same status. They are willing to cooperate with each other to maximize the use of their resources. In most other areas there is nothing to share because there is little if any difference in their resources. In this instance, however, a rudimentary type of differentiation exists: cooperation is based on a division of labor by time rather than function.[2] However, transfers rarely occur between low- and high-status institutions simply because one is filled to capacity. Unless lower class patients have need for some esoteric treatment the difference in cost and physical location tends to keep them in lower status institutions. Moreover, the middle- and upper-class patients of the high-status institutions usually refuse to be transferred to the lower status ones.

Inequality and Functional Differentiation

Much of social theory has stressed differentiation of function as a key prerequisite to cooperation. As our theoretical discussion of scarcity and interdependence indicated, complementary scarcities leading to interdependence are an important basis of cooperation. But what much of the analysis of interorganizational relations has not stressed is that inequality can be a primary basis of functional differentiation and cooperative interdependence. Moreover, inequality may be the source of functional differentiation rather than emerge from it. Perhaps this notion has been developed most explicitly by Peter Blau:

At first, all members of the collectivity compete against all others, but as status differences emerge in consequence of differential success in the initial competition, the object of the competition changes, and symbiotic exchange relations become differentiated from competitive ones. Those successful in the earlier stages of competition tend to compete later for dominant positions . . . while the unsuccessful ones cannot compete with them for dominance and become their exchange partners, who receive instrumental benefits in exchange for subordination and . . . support.[3]

Blau and Scott have specifically applied these notions to interorganizational relationships.[4] I do not want to argue that all differentiation of function is the result of inequality of power—but much of it is. Consequently, even a significant proportion of the integration that seems to emerge from differentiation of function may be indirectly attributable to inequality of power—which is, of course, one of the two basic types of simplification.

Clearly other aspects of the observed pattern of interorganizational linkages are directly related to differentiation of power, influence, and status. Perhaps the clearest example is the effect of inequality on status anxiety. While both Johnson and Bernstein have low status in the health system as a whole, they are still concerned about their relative status with respect to each other; each fears the other might gain some undue advantage from cooperative relations. Undoubtedly the personal ambitions and status concerns of the individuals involved are also relevant. This is illustrated by some of the tensions concerning the proposed merger of Johnson and Bernstein. One of our field workers recorded the following observations:

The administrator of Johnson, seems to be unresponsive to the community demands and acting in a very conservative fashion. . . . According to _____, she is not well liked and is insecure about her position, since she lacks a background in hospital administration. She seems to be particularly threatened by the proposed health park, since the administrator of Bernstein has had many more years of experience and would be a favorite if a new administrator were to be chosen for the new facility.

This interpretation is supported by two other pieces of information. The administrator of Bernstein does have considerably more experience than the administrator of Johnson. Moreover, in our interview, the Johnson administrator, Mrs. Helen Walker, brings up the issue of relative status: "Bernstein is not fully accredited in many areas. . . . We are fully accredited, and *having the better status, we can cooperate* with them and work with them in developing health care for our area" (emphasis added). Obviously, relative status seems to be an important consideration in Mrs. Walker's view, and she is careful to make clear which institution, in her opinion, has the higher status. Whether her evaluation is accurate is at least open to debate; what is apparent is that such statements are not likely to increase Bernstein's enthusiasm toward the proposed merger. In contrast, these issues have little effect on relationships between Mercy and Johnson because the status difference is so great. Mercy has no fears that Johnson is going to overtake it and Johnson has no illusions or aspirations in this regard.

Inequality of power—if we use the term to include command of resources—affects integration in yet another way. Communication, especially if it must hammer out the terms of joint activity through particularistic interaction, is time consuming and costly. Higher status institutions can much better afford the "communication cost" required to work out cooperative relationships. Many of the Mercy staff have major responsibilities in the area of interorganizational relationships and in turn have few, if any, responsibilities for carrying out the internal functions of the hospital. Such positions do not exist at Johnson. Institutions operating on a hand-to-mouth basis do not have resources for nonessential endeavors, even when these might improve their long-term position. This is not to say that all communication problems are due to scarcity or that communication cannot be improved without additional resources. But actors with relatively plentiful resources do have a greater chance of integrating additional activities because they can afford the "investment cost."

We shall consider other ways in which the equality-inequality dimension operates in the simplification process, but this must be postponed until we examine additional data.

Universalistic Rules

In addition to organizational inequality, the dimension of particularism-universalism has a significant effect on interorganizational relationships. In particularistic relationships, interaction is governed by characteristics of the actors and mutual sets of expectations—a type of abstraction—that are relatively special or unique to that specific relationship. In contrast, universalistic linkages are governed by abstract general standards relevant to many concrete relationships.

Earlier I argued that particularistic interaction is usually costly as a means of organizing instrumental activity; too high a proportion of the social time and energies available is spent on the interaction required for integration rather than on activity. However, once particularlistic relationships are established, they reduce the amount of subsequent interaction required to integrate additional joint activity. Consequently, already established interpersonal links play an important part in encouraging joint interorganizational activity. However, particularistic interaction even in the context of established relationships can still be a time-consuming way to integrate activity. Consequently more elaborate simplification mechanisms evolve. Typically one of the first mechanisms developed is universalistic norms; they allow a decision about a particular case to be based on a limited number of characteristics of that case.

The transfer of patients from hospitals with a shortage of beds to those with a surplus is a good example of such a procedure. The information required to decide whether a transfer is appropriate and possible requires only telephone communication. Moreover, the decision is based almost entirely on universalistic criteria: acuteness of medical need, residence of the patient and location of the institution, and availability of suitable facilities. Because cases are relatively standardized and decisions are based on universalistic criteria, no special particularistic relationship is required. A considerable number of hospitals roughly on the same prestige level participate more or less regularly in the transfer process. Hence there are cases where interorganizational interactions involve standardized cases decided on the basis of universalistic criteria. Such cases require no particularistic relationships or specialized decision-making mechanisms (such as authority structures or markets) to produce efficient interorganizational activity.[5]

Particularistic Relations

In contrast nearly all the other relationships described in this chapter are dependent on some element of particularism. The neurosurgeon at Mercy does not go to any hospital that requests his services, but only to Johnson, where a specific arrangement has been worked out. Dr. Ravel, the Johnson pathologist, is able to secure assistance from University Hospital only because of his personal relationships with members of the staff there. The transfer of patients from Johnson to Mercy for scanning procedures emerged out of a particular set of earlier experiences with the "whole body" machine. Dr. Mooreman, the chief of pediatrics for both Johnson and Bernstein, claims that the most important factor in securing the assistance of another institution is to personally know someone on the staff.

Two factors seem to lie behind the correlation between particularistic personal relations and interorganizational cooperation. First, particular personal relationships enable individuals to transform personal ties and exchanges into organizational transactions. That is, obligations "owed" to them personally can to some extent be used for organizational purposes. Dr. Mooreman's use of Mercy for certain laboratory tests because as an individual he is a member of the Mercy staff is one example. As we have seen, the Johnson pathologist often used this mechanism.

But a second, perhaps more important, mechanism is at work. Individuals with personal ties have in some sense established the grounding or framework for later interactions. In many areas of activity they have already developed sets of mutual understandings, so they know what to expect from one another. To the extent that the particularistic relationship involves respect or friendship it usually means that these expectations contain an element of mutual trust. Each party is reasonably sure that he can carry on additional interaction without being taken advantage of. Consequently, when such individuals interact in their organizational roles, their individual ties greatly reduce the interaction required to arrive at mutual understanding and agreement about the organizational issue at hand. In short, particularistic personal ties reduce the amount of time and energy required for interorganizational communication and agreement.

In a sense particularistic relationships and universalistic rules are alternative mechanisms for reducing the interaction needed for a transaction. In the first instance the standardized nature of the case and the universalistic rules governing such cases make possible the reaching of agreement with a minimum of interaction. There is already a cultural consensus about what should be done if a specialized event occurs. The two organizations need only communicate enough to establish that the case at hand conforms to the universal norms. In the second instance, the transaction is not governed by universal standardized norms. No cultural consensus exists that says the pathology department at one hospital should provide major resources to train the residents of another hospital. Only where the recipient institution is represented by an individual who can be depended on both to make proper use of such assistance and not to take advantage of the relationships does such an interorganizational relationship develop. University Medical School's rejection of Dr. Ravel's attempt to transform his link into a more explicit and formal interorganizational relationship is instructive in this respect. Dr. Ravel, as an individual, was seen as a deserving and trustworthy recipient of such assistance. Johnson Hospital, as an institution, was not defined as "dependable." Therefore, the chief of pathology at University Hospital was willing to be involved in an interorganizational relationship as long as it was based on a particularistic personal link; the expectations were dependable and acceptable. From his point of view this would not be the case if the relationship were transformed into a formal impersonal linkage. In the latter case neither the protection of universalistic norms nor particularistic relationships would apply.

Conclusions

The health system's institutionalized ideology calls for cooperation and coordination between organizations to maximize the efficiency of the overall system. At the same time this ideology denies the legitimacy of the most common social mechanisms used to obtain such an outcome in complex societies, that is, centralized authority and market competition. As a result much of the cooperation and coordination occurring in this sector are the result of relationships that evolve out of particularistic interaction. Such linkages are in some respects analogous to the interpersonal relationships in a neighborhood. But particularistic interaction between organizations is very time consuming and therefore costly. Moreover a consensus about the terms of a cooperative relationship is difficult when institutions are competing for organizational prestige or scarce resources. This chapter illustrates some of the linkages that tend to form between hospitals under these conditions.

Two factors seem especially important in determining whether linkages are likely to evolve. First interorganizational links are more likely to develop where there are first particularistic personal relationships—for the various reasons discussed earlier. However, for interorganizational transactions involving relatively standardized cases (for example, the referral and transfer of patients), relationships tend to be governed by universalistic norms, that is, rule systems. Moreover these rule systems are largely independent of an authority structure, because disagreement over how the rules should be applied is rare. For example, when a person lives at a certain address clearly within the catchment area of a particular hospital, there is seldom disagreement about which institution has responsibility. Such rule systems not only operate independently of authority structures but also depend much less on particularistic relationships. Stated slightly differently, both particularistic relationships and universalistic rules provide actors with sets of common abstractions. These shared abstractions may be categories used primarily for communication, or they may be norms and expectations specifying patterns of appropriate behavior. In both cases their presence reduces the amount of interaction required to integrate subsequent joint activities.

Second, interorganizational integration and links are most likely to occur between organizations significantly different in terms of power and status. Inequality of power reduces the level of interaction required for two actors to work out an integrated relationship. This inequality may reduce the interaction required because an actor explicitly forces a pattern of behavior on another. A clear inequality of power also reduces the "jockeying for position" that frequently occurs when actors of more nearly equal status attempt to integrate joint activities.

In short, the processes producing simplification and therefore increasing the probability of integrated joint activity can be boiled down to common abstractions—which may be either particularistic or universalistic—and inequality of power.

Chapter Six

SYMBIOTIC INEQUALITY

The last three chapters have focused on the second set of factors affecting interorganizational relationships: the ease or difficulty in negotiating a relationship. We have considered how various mechanisms (for example, authority structures, markets, universalistic rules, and particularistic relationships) simplify the establishment of links and the coordination of activity. We have also discussed the conditions encouraging the use of one of these mechanisms rather than another. But a recurring theme in all these chapters has been interorganizational inequality. In addition to the role it plays in the simplification process, it is a crucial aspect of the first set of factors, resource dependencies. Inequality focuses on the relative success and failure of organizations in the struggle for resources. This chapter pulls together and analyzes the material on inequality dispersed through the previous chapters. The intent is to refine the resource dependency perspective, focusing especially on why and how powerful organizations limit their exercise of power and provide assistance to less powerful organizations.

Feudal noblemen not infrequently exploited their peasants; rarely did they abuse them to the point of starvation or death. While Christian virtue played its role, momentary reflection suggests an additional reason for this restraint; dead peasants produced few rents and were exceedingly ineffective as soldiers and servants. The long-term maintenance of power and privilege required a keen sensitivity to both the possibilities and limitations of exploitation. Moreover, noblemen performed vital services by protecting their peasants from exploitation by others and by keeping order within the community. For inequality to be maintained it had to be a symbiotic inequality. These characteristics of feudalism are found in many systems of inequality. Let us see to what degree they apply to urban health care facilities.

THE NECESSITY OF CONTROLLING A VITAL RESOURCE

The underlying basis of most of the interorganizational inequality in this urban neighborhood rests upon the difference between desirable and undesirable patients. Desirable patients have at least one of the following characteristics: (1) they are able to pay the full charges for the services they receive; (2) their ailment is medically interesting; or (3) they utilize specialized staff or equipment.

From earlier discussions it should be apparent that a central and crucial problem for high-status hospitals is to secure an adequate number of desirable patients and limit the proportion of undesirable patients. This ability is not a sufficient condition for a metropolitan hospital to acquire or maintain high status, but it is, with rare exceptions, a necessary condition for doing so. Let us review briefly, therefore, some of the mechanisms we have identified for securing such an outcome. The most obvious is the ambulance service. But equally important is the "farming-out system." As was pointed out in chapter 5 the sending of patients from Johnson to Mercy for esoteric services helps Mercy justify expensive equipment and highly specialized personnel. All these mechanisms also contribute to a wider and more interesting array of "teaching material." Another means of limiting undesirable outpatients is to give poor service. The human quality of Mercy's outpatient care is very little better than Johnson's and is probably worse than that at Bernstein. If the service were better the OPD would be even more overwhelmed with patients. This is not to suggest that Mercy deliberately and consciously plans long waiting periods, impersonal treatment, and crowded facilities. It does mean they have little motivation to improve; the demand for services would only increase from the portion of the population least able to pay. Moreover they have generally had the power to resist the demands of their clients and outsiders that the human quality of these services be improved.

THE DILEMMA OF EXPLOITATION

Yet high-status institutions are confronted with a dilemma. If they are too successful in securing desirable patients and keeping undesirable patients at low-status institutions, the financial condition of such institutions is likely to become intolerable. Voluntary hospitals such as Johnson may be forced to close. Public hospitals such as Bernstein may be able to remain open, but the cost to the public treasury becomes very high, and services deteriorate even further. Such an outcome can cause the legitimacy of the health care system, including the voluntary hospitals, to be called into serious question. In short, the high-status institutions must ensure that low-status ones continue to exist and function in a more or less acceptable manner. What would happen to Mercy if Johnson Hospital closed? To repeat the words of the Mercy administrator, "What in God's name would we do with 100,000 more outpatients!" He knows the answer to this rhetorical question and, for understandable reasons, does not relish the possibility. Given the structure of feudal society, there must be peasants if there are to be noblemen. Given the structure of Fairmont's health care system—and certain aspects of our broader society—there must be a Johnson if there is to be a Mercy. In larger American cities of today (with current health care patterns as they are) maintaining high-quality hospitals would be very difficult if low-quality hospitals did not take care of a substantial portion of the undesirable patients. Too many people are simply unable to pay the cost of high-quality medical care as currently organized and provided.

One can easily be overly cynical about the relationship between the low- and high-quality institutions. Certainly many of the linkages exist because they are of mutual benefit. On the other hand, most of the physicians and staff at hospitals like Mercy are concerned about the plight of low-status hospitals and the poor people they serve. Like many middle-class people in our society they "do what they can" to alleviate the problems of the less fortunate—so long as their basic activities and privileges are not threatened. In short, both vested interest and altruism are operating in this situation. While many of the workers at the lower status hospitals harbor resentments about the way the health system is organized, they also appreciate that those in higher status institutions often go out of their way to be of assistance. Clearly the ambulance driver resents the well-to-do patients' carefully avoiding Johnson. On the other hand, when Dr. Martinez characterizes Johnson's relationship to Mercy he says, "From my point of view I have a beautiful relationship with them." He perceives them to be sympathetic and helpful to Johnson's needs. The crucial point is that the difficulties existing between low- and high-status institutions are not due primarily to hostile or even selfish attitudes on the part of the staffs involved. If anything the ideology and attitudes help mitigate the problems and make the best of a bad situation. The norms calling for interorganizational cooperation and coordination are not totally window dressing.

Reinhard Bendix's discussion of Weber's concept of "patriarchalism" illustrates the point that normative limitations are a common feature of informal and particularly traditional domination:

. . . filial piety for the person of the master is combined with reverence for the sanctity of tradition, and while the first element greatly enhances the power of the master, the second tends to keep it within bounds.

This double emphasis on the arbitrary power of the master and the limitation of that power by sacred tradition is a basic characteristic of traditional domination in all its forms.[1]

In short, exploitation is held in check by a combination of two factors. First even low-status subordinates are usually more valuable when they are alive—dead peasants and defunct ghetto hospitals are not very useful. Second, the privileged are reluctant to openly violate traditional doctrinal norms such as noblesse oblige—in this context the ideological claim of the medical professions and democratic societies that all "deserving" persons will receive a basic level of health care.

INEQUALITY AND THE COST OF EMULATION

There is another negative consequence of interorganizational inequality not due to exploitation—even in its symbiotic form. Rather it can probably best be understood by means of the concept of reference group. The basic notion is that an actor patterns his behavior after some group of actors whom he holds in high esteem or at least would like to emulate.[2]

In our context the most important example is the effect of the dual system on the definition of adequate health care. What is considered adequate is pegged to what the upper middle and upper classes can afford. Johnson must arrange to farm out scanning procedures because these are now defined as essential to proper medical care in the Fairmont area. But one wonders if medical care at Johnson might not actually be better on the average if resources were invested in additional staff and more basic equipment and supplies. This is not really an option, however. The higher status institutions define what constitutes adequate care; the technology, procedures, and organization they use are the model that poorer institutions imitate. This may actually reduce the level of care. An analogy to this problem is the tendency of developing nations to adopt inappropriate technology. For example, in some situations more roads can be built and maintained cheaper by organizing vast numbers of laborers to work with picks and shovels than by importing expensive power machinery. The latter are fantastically efficient—but only in an economy where labor costs are high and equipment maintenance costs are low. When such machines are operated in underdeveloped areas they can actually reduce productivity because of the energy and resources required to operate a technology incompatible with the rest of the technological and social environment.

In addition, the unequal distribution of income and wealth may contribute to the inefficient use of the health resources available to the lower classes. More precisely it introduces another divergence in the interests of health care professionals and the patients they serve. Doctors and health care administrators tend to be judged and evaluated by how closely their activities and organizations match those of the high-status institutions. In terms of the interests of the clients of low-status institutions, this leads to inefficient use of the already inadequate resources.

INEQUALITY, PLURALISM, AND CONFLICT

Another characteristic of this particular instance of symbiotic inequality is striking: the relative lack of open public conflict. This is particularly surprising in light of the obvious conflicts of interest between institutions. At least three factors contribute to this. First, Mercy's status and power is so secure relative to Johnson or Bernstein that open conflict is probably more of a threat to the low-status institutions. Even the prospect that the ambulance service might be reorganized in such a way as to make Johnson's financial situation untenable did not result in open conflict. Instead, Mercy used its influence with the city to secure what it wanted and to protect at least the essential interests of Johnson. Johnson was virtually passive during the process. Second, the staff at Johnson— at least those with regular outside contact—perceive the staff of the high-status institutions to be on the whole sympathetic, if not overly responsive, to their problems. Third, and probably most important, Johnson's links involve "voluntary" exchanges with a plurality of other institutions. For example, neither Johnson nor Mercy is under any formal or legal obligation to cooperate with each other, though the ideology of coordination places them under moral obligation to do so. This is true for nearly all of Johnson's links. Linkages are usually limited, therefore, to matters about which there exists a set of reasonably congruent expectations. If serious conflict and disagreement over the appropriate terms of a potential linkage arise, the relationship simply does not come to fruition. Here is the crucial point: when voluntaristic relationships emerge primarily out of particularistic interaction between a plurality of actors they tend to be relatively free of open conflict. This is so precisely because the institutional structures make it possible to limit relationships to areas of agreement. There are many parallels with the market here. Johnson is "free" to establish linkages wherever they can get the best deal. Consequently, they send patients for scans and brain surgery to Mercy but send cardiology patients to Mellon and look to the city health department and University Medical School for support in pathology. Because exchanges and relationships are diffused across a number of actors, disagreements and hostilities are diffused. Johnson can have no complaint; it has gotten more than it has any legal right to demand and supposedly the "best deal" available. If Johnson is dissatisfied with a particular relationship, it has the formal right—if not the actual opportunity—to establish a more satisfactory linkage elsewhere. At least in the context of modern societies, symbiotic inequality is probably most stable when it is based on voluntaristic relationships between the uppers and lowers rather than linkages fixed by law or tradition. This will become more apparent when we examine the data in Part III.

SYMBIOTIC INEQUALITY AND MERGER

The reliance on informal inequality suggests that the resource dependency model needs further specification. Pfeffer and Salancik argue that dominant organizations absorb their environment—either by growth or merger—to manage interdependence and reduce uncertainty.[3] Organizations supposedly move toward vertical integration (that is, acquire organizations producing critical inputs for existing activities) when exchange has become problematic. For example, Mercy attempts to develop an ambulance service to secure more trauma patients and to reduce uncertainty about the mix of desirable and undesirable patients. In contrast, the theory predicts horizontal expansion (that is, the absorption of units with essentially the same function as the "parent" unit) when there is a need to reduce competitive uncertainty.

But how do we explain Mercy's significant efforts to assist and stabilize Johnson on the one hand and their total lack of interest in formally absorbing Johnson on the other? The motivation for both vertical and horizontal absorption would seem to be operating here. On the one hand Johnson performs a vital service for Mercy by serving clients the latter had rather not have. Moreover, there is considerable uncertainty about how long Johnson will be able to continue to do this. On the other hand, Johnson does drain off some of the desirable clients Mercy would like. Why does Mercy not take over Johnson? No laws forbid this.

The reason for Mercy's reticence is that functions and activities vary significantly in the prestige and rewards they bring to those who carry them out. It is not enough that an actor be highly dependent on a particular function. The actor must also perceive that the function will bring rewards that will not decrease the overall standing in the stratification structure. When such rewards are not anticipated the dominant actor will try to accomplish two things: (1) ensure that someone with a distinct separate identity performs the low-status function, and (2) maintain significant indirect and informal control over the lower status actor. None of this is to basically reject the resource dependence approach. To predict whether interdependence and uncertainty will lead to formal merger or informal manipulation a further specification of the resource dependence model is needed; when the direct rewards of the new functions or activities are significantly below those received for existing functions we would expect the dominant organization to avoid formal merger.

SUMMARY

In the last four chapters we have analyzed the way in which interorganizational relationships are ordered between health care institutions in an urban neighborhood. The institutional context calls upon such organizations to coordinate their activities in the interest of the wider social welfare. At the same time these institutional structures prohibit, or at least discourage, reliance on the most common social mechanisms for accomplishing such coordination—competitive markets and centralized authority structures. Hence, what coordination exists is due largely to the linkages emerging from particularistic interaction; to limited special-purpose authority structures, such as the city ambulance system; and to highly imperfect quasi-markets. Cutting across and affecting all these mechanisms are the more general factors of common abstractions and inequality. The first is embodied in well-established interorganizational links and in networks of interpersonal links that underlie the interorganizational network. The latter is more evident and prevalent in the structure of interorganizational stratification.

This system of organizations is pluralistic in two senses. First, there is a complex mixture of different mechanisms of integration; the means of simplification and integration are clearly multiple. Second, the situation is pluralistic in the more traditional political sense. There are a plurality of actors who are partially committed to the public interest and yet pursue, with varying degrees of vigor and effectiveness, their individual self-interest. Moreover they are not subject to a unified structure of authority. From this complex mixture of actors and mechanisms of integration the following three striking structural features have emerged: a pattern of organizational stratification that is in large degree a two-class system, one set of institutions for the poor and another primarily (though not exclusively) for the middle and upper classes. Equally important and more easily overlooked is a set of crucial cooperative relationships between low-status and high-status institutions. Finally there is an eagerness on the part of the dominant institution to stabilize the activities of the low-status institution without becoming directly identified with those activities. These relationships mitigate the harshest elements of the dual structure but at the same time stabilize and perpetuate it. This pattern of relationships can be appropriately characterized by the term *symbiotic inequality*.

RELATED PERSPECTIVES

The notion of symbiotic inequality is not new, though I am not aware of the term's being used previously. As we have seen, Peter Blau has argued that a very common pattern in the development of social relationships is competition, inequality, functional differentiation, and finally symbiotic exchange. A second relevant theoretical argument has been developed by Gerhard E. Lenski in the context of analyzing macro structures of stratification.[4] He suggests that two basic principles govern the distribution of valued resources. One is power; the most powerful actors demand and receive a greatly disproportionate share of the resources available to the collectivity. But this first process is mitigated by a second principle of distribution, need. The minimal needs of most actors are met even when they are virtually powerless. If this were not the case the powerless would soon be exterminated and the privileged members of society would have to take over their activities. Lenski's argument is intended to apply primarily to the relationship between subgroupings of individuals and families. But certainly the basic argument parallels our own findings regarding the relationships between health care institutions. The notion of symbiotic inequality is intended to call attention to the dual aspect of most stratification. Relationships of inequality most often involve elements both of power and need, exploitation and support.

Finally, there is at least an analogy between Wallerstein's basic argument about the emergence and operation of the modern world economic system and the data presented here.[5] Wallerstein argues that for modern industrial societies to develop it was essential that there be a worldwide division of labor, the developing core nations specializing in and monopolizing the more rewarding functions, while less rewarding activities were forced on weak peripheral societies. Secondly, he says that an essential feature of this arrangement was the discarding of the old world empires and the handling of international relations by more indirect and informal means. England of the sixteenth century followed this course, while Spain clung to her old empire. The former course was clearly the more successful. Wallerstein's argument suggests that there are sometimes great benefits for dominant actors if they can (1) impose an informal division of labor that reserves the most rewarding functions for themselves and (2) maintain dominance over the system without taking formal authority (and responsibility).

That the findings of this study are congruent with these three basic theoretical perspectives does at least suggest that the structures and processes described are not simply idiosyncratic patterns relevant only to the particular case we have focused upon. Now we turn to the institutional context within which we have found the structure of symbiotic inequality and ask what the relationship is between that context and the type of stratification we have observed.

Chapter Seven

INSTITUTIONAL CONTEXT

This chapter focuses on the third set of factors having a crucial impact on interorganizational relationships: the institutional context. But first let us briefly review the main findings of the earlier chapters. With respect to factors affecting the ease or difficulty in negotiating relationships, we found that, relatively speaking, there was a paucity of the usual simplification mechanisms of markets and centralized bureaucratic authority. Those present tended to be highly imperfect and bastardized. In the absence of authority structures and markets there was a heavy reliance on particularistic relationships and informal dominance to integrate interorganizational relationships. With respect to the allocation of resources between organizations, there existed a dual system of institutions: one set of low-status institutions and another set of high-status ones. While the high-status institutions were clearly dominant and those of low-status were often in an extremely dependent position, extensive assistance was given to the low-status institutions because of the process of what I have called symbiotic inequality. Finally, while there was much talk about the need to formally increase coordination and cooperation, especially between low-status institutions, little ever happened in this regard.

To a significant degree this state of affairs results from the outcome in the struggle for resources engaged in by these particular organizations. But these struggles have not occurred in a strictly neighborhood or even city context. They were bounded and channeled by ideologies, norms, and power structures operating on the societal level. This chapter describes and specifies the institutional context which allowed and abetted the outcome so far depicted.[1]

THE SIGNIFICANCE OF THE INSTITUTIONAL CONTEXT

The structure of relationships both within and between organizations is affected not only by the needs of the organization and the power it might have over its immediate environment but also by broader institutionalized normative pressures. Many companies avoid outright monopolies, not because of an innate aversion to such activity (or even because they are unable to absorb their competitors) but because of antitrust laws and the sanctions they might bring. A long tradition in organizational analysis, known as the institutional approach, stresses the connections between the larger society and the specific organization.[2] Stinchcombe provided the seminal statement exploring the relationship between organizations and the broader institutionalized social structure.[3] For example, the precise activities and internal structure of organizations are in part determined by the particular period in which they were founded, even when other factors such as basic goals, functions, and location are more or less constant.[4] Similarly, different historical and cultural backgrounds can produce significantly different patterns for organizing what is, technically speaking, the same activity.[5] More recently Meyer and Rowan have provided an important statement about the significance of institutionalized myths and ceremonies—rather than simply rational efficiency pressures—in determining organizational structure and success.[6] In slightly different terms Warren has elaborated a congruent and parallel argument applied specifically to interorganizational relationships. For example, he argues that domain consensus between organizations is normally regulated much more by the acceptance of generalized institutionalized norms, more or less the same across localities, than by actual interaction, negotiation, and conflict between particular organizations.[7]

Recent interorganizational analysis has stressed the importance of "mandated" interorganizational relations, namely, those required by some explicit higher authority.[8] Most of the attention has been given to relationships in some sense legally mandated. Laws requiring that two organizations maintain cooperative relations are one aspect of the institutional context. Antitrust laws forbidding organizations to cooperate are another aspect of that context. But perhaps more important are nonlegal, conventional ideologies and normative pressures. By paying special attention to these less formal structures this book examines a broader array of institutionalized normative pressures than is usually considered in the literature.

In my opinion these institutionalized factors are extremely important in understanding interorganizational relationships between health and welfare institutions. This is particularly true with respect to the long history of complaints about the lack of interorganizational coordination. In this chapter I elaborate, in admittedly brief and simplified form, what seem to be the key institutionalized ideologies relevant to interorganizational relationships in the United States. These descriptions are the background or field against which networks of specific organizations must be viewed.

COMPETITION AND COORDINATION

There have tended to be two institutionalized answers or models for the appropriate means of interrelating organizations. Stated another way, two primary simplification mechanisms are institutionalized, each with its own advocates. One model stresses the importance of *competition* between organizations as the means to efficiency. This emphasis implicitly, and often explicitly, assumes that such organizations participate in a market system regulated by prices. The other model calls for *coordination* of relations between organizations and usually assumes the presence of some type of authority structure—typically, though not necessarily, a centralized and bureaucratic one.

The significance of these two different modes of organizing productive activity and interrelating organizations has been magnified to the point that they can be used to characterize, in an admittedly oversimplified fashion, whole societies and even cultures. Market competition is the essence of laissez faire capitalism. Centralized planning and coordination is the essence of state socialism.[9]

These two modes of organization and ideology also help identify a major differentiation within American society. Competition is the legitimate mode in the private sector; coordination is the byword in the public sector. This difference is in turn linked to the cultural assumptions made about what goals are legitimate for the actors in each of the two sectors. In the private area the key actors are business firms, and we assume that to a very large degree they will and should pursue their own self-interest. Competition is not only allowed, it is normatively and legally required, as Chamber of Commerce rhetoric and antitrust laws indicate. In the public sector the opposite is true. Government, quasi-governmental public agencies, and "nonprofit" organizations are the key actors. They cannot legitimately seek to enrich themselves at the expense of others. Rather, they are charged with pursuing the public interests. Moreover, they are expected to coordinate their activities and avoid competing with one another. Not only do the definitions of legitimate means and ends vary, but also each sector has differing definitions of what constitutes a pathology. The chief source of inefficiency in the market is supposedly restricted competition. Inefficiency arises when monopolies develop and illicit coordination is substituted for competition. The opposite is the case for public and nonprofit agencies. The chief source of inefficiency is seen as lack of coordination, and wasteful competition and conflict. Few criticisms or exposés of government inefficiency proceed very far before they begin to discuss "lack of coordination."

Like most ideologies these two models describe idealized situations. Even in the most competitive sectors of business there are often considerable cooperation and coordination between competitors.[10] On the other hand, public organizations supposedly committed to cooperation and coordination frequently engage in extensive competition and even open conflict. But of equal interest is that the degree of disparity between ideology and actuality varies for different sectors of U.S. society.[11] When we consider the degree of congruence between ideology and actuality in terms of competition and coordination, four situations are suggested. These are shown in the typology presented on the next page.

Three of the cells in this typology refer to forms of interorganizational relations commonly recognized and widely discussed. The *market system* is the world of farmers and small businesses: hardware stores, neighborhood bars and cafes, washaterias, beauty parlors, TV repair shops, bicycle shops. These organizations are related to one another largely in terms of the pricing system of a competitive market and have been exten-

The Degree of Congruence Between the Ideological and the Actual Means for Interrelating Organizations in American Society

		ACTUALITY	
		Competition	Coordination
IDEOLOGY	Competition (private sector)	Market system	Industrial system
	Coordination (public sector)	Welfare system	Government system

sively analyzed by traditional microeconomics. The *government system* transforms most interorganizational relationships into intraorganizational ties. That is, formal structures of authority in large degree specify who is responsible for resolving conflicts and ordering relationships between agencies.[12] The *industrial system* is the world of large corporations.[13] Here the virtue and legitimacy of competition is loudly and repeatedly proclaimed. But a considerable gap exists between the public litanies and the structural realities. While agreement is rare about the details of how this sector operates, it is widely recognized that competition is significantly restricted and that various forms of indirect and implicit coordination are important.

The fourth type of interorganizational relationship is particularly characteristic of what might be called the *welfare system*. Organizations in this sector of our society are responsible for providing services that are neither the clear responsibility of the government nor usually provided by profit-oriented firms. Health, social services, and, to some extent, education are the activities most characteristic of the organizations operating in this sector.[14]

With respect to interorganizational relationships within the welfare system, and more particularly the health sector, we find the mirror image of the situation in the industrial sector. The accepted ideology is coordination, but frequently the actuality is either disorganization or outright competition. As in the industrial sector, the structural prerequisites assumed by the ideology are largely absent. In the industrial system there are too few actors for the operation of a competitive market in the classical sense. In the welfare system there are few authority or even communication structures through which coordination can be obtained. Rather the system is composed of a multitude of largely independent organizations subject to relatively little external control, except for the broad guidelines laid down by licensing and accrediting agencies and the generally limited coordination provided by what historically have been rather weak planning agencies.

PLURALISM AND PARTICULARISTIC INTERACTION

The institutionalized context of the welfare system seems to produce at least two outcomes. On the one hand, observers continually complain about lack of coordination and fragmentation of services. For example, an HEW report notes: "The catch-as-catch-can structure of our unplanned medical care system is comprised of conflicting and duplicating activities on the one hand and gaps in service on the other."[15] The second result is that social analysts have drawn heavily on the model of political pluralism in an attempt to understand the operation of the health care system in particular and interorganizational relations in general.

Aiken and Hage are perhaps most explicit about this parallel:

The models of pluralistic societies described by Tocqueville and more recently by Kornhauser underscore the importance of autonomous and competing organizations for viable democratic processes. Such theoretical models assume that the processes of conflict as well as cooperation inhere in social reality. Recent American social theory has been criticized for its excessive emphasis on a static view of social processes and for failing to include conflict in its conceptual models. The study of interorganizational relationships appears to be one area which can appropriately incorporate the processes of both conflict and cooperation. Therefore, the concept of organizational interdependence becomes a critical analytical tool for understanding this process.[16]

The pluralistic model is also implicit in the work of Clark and the early work of Warren.[17]

The cardinal idea in this model is that collective decisions are worked out through extensive interaction involving an array of actors. This interaction results in mutual adjustment or accommodation between the various actors. On the political level these actors are usually some type of interest group: labor unions, ethnic groups, corporations, farm organizations, etc. In the health sector the actors are the various institutions and organizations: hospitals, clinics, city health departments, local social service agencies, community committees and councils, and funding agencies such as HEW. Collective "decisions" are made and activities are coordinated through a process analogous to the mutual adjustment described by the model of political pluralism.

I want to suggest that both the political pluralism model and the adaptation used for interorganizational analysis are special cases of the process I have earlier described as particularistic interaction. In pluralism, however, the actors are primarily organizations and other collectivities rather than individual persons. As with individuals, organizations integrate their activities through more or less direct particularistic interaction involving mutual adjustments, the development of relatively stable expectations, coalition formation, etc.

THE CRITIQUE OF PLURALISM

Political pluralism has been repeatedly criticized on two grounds.[18] First it is accused of understating or ignoring persistent inequalities of power and privilege. Second, it is seen as highly inefficient and time consuming leading to endless delays and stalemates. More recently a related criticism has been added. It is seen as a means of thwarting or drastically limiting significant change; an endless series of incremental reform efforts produces little or no effect.

These same criticisms are leveled at the health care system. Robert Alford and Roland Warren have both argued that most reform efforts in health and welfare are blunted or deflected despite the appearance of considerable innovation. According to them the basic interests of established organizations are rarely threatened. Warren argues that even when this occurs the system as a whole—as distinct from the interests of any one organization or group, even a very powerful one—remains largely unchanged.[19]

The earlier chapters show that, at least with respect to this research site, the first criticism of pluralism is largely correct; significant and persistent inequalities exist between health care institutions. But perhaps more important I have tried to fill in some of the details by indicating how the two-class system operates, particularly some of the ways in which high-status institutions maintain their dominance and how their dominance is mitigated through symbiotic inequality. In the next two chapters I attempt a similar task with respect to the second and third criticisms of pluralism. There are two questions to be answered. First, why stalemate and conflict, rather than integrated cooperative relations, occur? Second, what determines which of these two outcomes, stalemate or open conflict, is most likely?

Before we proceed, two additional points are required. I have suggested that the characteristics of interorganizational relations among the Southside's health care institutions are in part due to the institutionalized ideologies and norms governing such relationships. More specifically, I have shown that the ideology applied to the welfare system—a stress on coordination on the one hand and autonomy on the other—leads to a situation analogous to political pluralism. The ways this institutional context is similar to and different from other sectors of the society have also been indicated. We have not, however, explored why these particular ideological formulas are institutionalized for the welfare sector. In this chapter, the ideological formulas have been used as an independent rather than a dependent variable. Later I offer some theoretical speculations about why the institutional context takes the form it does.

The second and related point is a caveat. The institutionalized ideological and normative context is an important determinant of the form interorganizational relationships take. But this emphasis needs qualification. David Mechanic claims that health care delivery seems fragmented and inadequately coordinated in nearly all societies.[20] He suggests this is in part rooted in the highly specialized nature of contemporary medical knowledge and technology. Undoubtedly this is true; the ideologies characteristic of American society are not the sole or even primary determinant of the fragmentation and inequality. On the other hand these problems vary considerably across societies and are not due solely to the technical nature of modern medicine. One must be careful not to attribute too much to the power of ideology and norms. But at the same time the institutional context must be analyzed if we are to adequately understand interorganizational relationships.

PART III

Chapter Eight

PLURALISTIC REFORM:
A COMPREHENSIVE COMMUNITY
HEALTH CENTER

Chapters 3–5 focused primarily on the means of interorganizational integration and their consequences for inequality. In contrast, this part of the book looks at some of the major impediments to interorganizational integration, namely, social conflict and what I call neutralization—the inability to take action because of high levels of interorganizational complexity.[1] These impediments are observed in the context of an attempt to reform the pluralistic urban health care system described in the earlier chapters. A key purpose of the reform is to reduce the inequalities characteristic of that system. In Part II inequality was seen primarily as a latent consequence of the modes of interorganizational integration. In Part III the focus is turned around; neutralization and social conflict are in many respects the latent consequences of attempts to reduce inequality.

First, this chapter introduces the data about interorganizational links relevant to a satellite neighborhood health center. Then the focus shifts to the role of the managing board of that satellite center, the Southside Health Committee. This allows us to consider an example of community participation in neighborhood health organizations. The purpose of this chapter is solely descriptive. The next chapter analyzes the key sources of the neutralization and social conflict described. Also analyzed is why high-status institutions become involved in such conflict-filled relationships. Taken as a unit, chapters 8 and 9 identify some of the key consequences of creating comprehensive health centers as a reform strategy.

COMMUNITY HEALTH CENTER

The Heightsville Community Health Center (HCHC) is a comprehensive community health clinic that is a satellite of Mercy Hospital. The words "comprehensive," "community," and "satellite" symbolize important features of the institution's interorganizational relationships. In this context, "community" implies community participation and consequently an increase in the number of interorganizational actors and the complexity of the decision-making process. Even more interorganizational linkages and complexities are implied by the notion of "comprehensive," which means the clinic tries to meet the full array of the individual's health needs. Since a neighborhood center cannot have all the staff and facilities necessary for health needs in a modern society, this notion implies extensive interorganizational links. Finally, "satellite" implies subservience to an external authority but also an autonomous identity and therefore further complexities. While satellites are ultimately under the authority and control of some parent organization, they usually have a separate and distinctive organizational identity and a high degree of autonomy in some areas. As we shall see, this structural schizophrenia has a number of important consequences. To identify some of the general characteristics of satellites and the complexities this type of organization tends to spawn we now examine in some detail the Heightsville Community Health Center (HCHC).

The Setting and the Actors

HCHC's purpose is to provide comprehensive health care to low-income residents; 60,000 people are estimated to reside in the center's official catchment area. During the study the center had about 15,000 registered patients, and more than 63,000 patient encounters (that is, more or less, visits) annually. To care for these people the center has a staff of approximately 170 people ranging from surgeons to janitors.

HCHC occupies the second floor of a relatively new and attractive building in the mode of monotonous-municipal-modern. The center contains a little more than 8,000 square feet, a space grossly inadequate for the needs. A row of chairs along the edge of the hall serves as the "waiting room." Original estimates indicated HCHC would need approximately three times this much space. The outcome is serious overcrowding. Despite this, HCHC is a relatively pleasant and humane place, compared to many other public health facilities for the poor. About 60 percent of the patients are Spanish speaking, about 20 percent are black, and the rest are lower class whites of mixed ethnic background. To be eligible for service at HCHC, a person must reside within the catchment area and be "on welfare" and/or eligible for Medicaid or Medicare.

HCHC was in a sense founded by Dr. John Warren, an energetic and entrepreneurial assistant director at Mercy. From the very early stages of HCHC's conception, Warren worked with a variety of community leaders in the area where the center was eventually established. A proposal written under his leadership was funded by the U.S. Office of Economic Opportunity (OEO). Mercy was the "grantee" and had full financial and administrative responsibility for the program. However, the money was channeled through a "delegate agency," the city government's Neighborhood Development Office (NDO). Supposedly the function of this procedure was to coordinate HCHC with other community development activities. Probably its more latent purpose was to gain the support and cooperation of local officials and politicians.

OEO approved the proposal contingent upon the development of a neighborhood advisory council. Initially the city's NDO formed the council by appointing about a dozen neighborhood people; they were individuals who had been working in other community development programs and/or were vocal about such matters. This group became the nucleus of the Southside Health Committee (SHC). Later SHC was expanded with representatives from a large number of local institutions and organizations: settlement houses, churches, political clubs, and the like. The powers and responsibilities of the Southside Health Committee were quite ambiguous, and as we shall see, this created no small amount of confusion and conflict.

The fifth member of the cast—so far there is (1) OEO, (2) the city's Neighborhood Development Office, (3) Mercy, and (4) the Southside Health Committee—is the city's health department. Like most organizations, especially governmental bureaucracies the health department was "uptight" about some new upstart's treading on their domain. For many years the health department had operated a series of neighborhood preventive health centers. Seven years before HCHC was organized, the city built a new center in the very neighborhood HCHC proposed to serve. Because of budget cuts this new health department building tended to be underutilized. To add insult to injury the OEO-funded center proposed taking over a significant proportion of the floor space in this new building. The department was not diametrically opposed to the center, but they insisted they should have a larger role than simply leasing space to HCHC. A contract between HCHC (or more accurately Mercy) and the health department was proposed that gave the latter certain formal responsibilities—including a clause that said the health officer would be responsible for administering the project. However, as contract negotiations developed, the health officer was not granted any budgetary powers and his main responsibility was for the maintenance of the building. Thus the scope of the health department's involvement reminds one of Panama's former titular sovereignty over the Canal Zone: largely a symbolic device with little if any actual authority. The final irony of the labored negotiations is that the contract has never been signed, despite the fact that HCHC has been located on the second floor of the department's building for over five years—rent free.

The sixth and last main character (more accurately set of characters) is the staff of the HCHC. In some formal sense the members of the staff are Mercy's employees and therefore could be considered agents of that institution. They do, however, have a distinct identity and a special status in relation to Mercy. The most important distinction is that the staff was employed specifically to work at HCHC. Many of the physicians do not have admitting privileges at Mercy, which definitely implies that they are considered to have lesser qualifications than the hospital's regular attending physicians. Given this relatively large and diverse set of main actors, it is not surprising that some complex problems arose.

A Satellite Relationship

HCHC is a satellite of Mercy. As the word satellite implies, HCHC is at the periphery rather than the core of Mercy's activities. While Mercy initiated the project and has legal, fiscal, and administrative control of the Center, HCHC is quite marginal to the core of the hospital's activities. To quote a member of the Mercy medical board:

I get the impression that the consensus would be that the HCHC is a marginal or peripheral activity which is necessary I would guess in the city at present. I don't believe many of the physicians in the hospital center spend much time considering what the problems of HCHC are, and look on it as a relatively remote function.

Yet Mercy initiated the project and has legal, fiscal, and administrative responsibility and control. One of Mercy's responsibilities under the terms of their contract with OEO, and later HEW, is to maintain a high quality of medical care. The primary mechanism for accomplishing this is the selection of the medical staff, the implicit assumption being that a qualified staff will themselves see that high standards are maintained.

In selecting personnel the first question is whether they are qualified to be staff members of HCHC. The second is whether they are, in addition, qualified to be members of the Mercy attending staff. The main privilege of this second distinction is the right to admit private patients at Mercy. In the eyes of Mercy and many teaching hospitals, this criterion separates the sheep from the goats. Except for the pediatricians, the majority of HCHC physicians are goats; they lack the professional stature necessary to become full members of the Mercy staff. The whole question of staff accreditation is, of course, a rather touchy issue. It is subject to more or less continuous negotiation between the hospital and the HCHC physicians, both on an individual and a collective level.

Another important aspect of the satellite relationship is Mercy's fiscal responsibility for the program; the money from the federal government comes to Mercy. Ultimately the hospital's board of trustees has final authority over expenditures. Therefore, despite HCHC's relatively high degree of independence and the hospital's generally low level of interest in the program, Mercy maintains a very high level of residual power and therefore ultimate control of the situation.

The first two functions of Mercy—financial affairs and selection of staff—could in principle be executed by HCHC itself. But Mercy performs other important functions that HCHC could not do autonomously. These can be grouped under the category of back-up services, the most obvious being inpatient care. Unless the clinic is transformed into a hospital per se, the commitment to comprehensive care requires a regularized arrangement with another institution for patients who require inpatient care. Mercy provides this critical back-up function, and in this respect the special satellite relationship is an important asset to HCHC.

Emergency care is another valuable back-up service performed by Mercy. When HCHC is not open or in life-threatening emergencies, patients are instructed to report to the Mercy emergency room. Not only do HCHC physicians avoid the inconvenience of unscheduled middle-of-the-night and weekend interruptions, but HCHC saves money also. Even though Mercy bills the center for emergency services to its patients, these charges are considerably less than the cost of HCHC's providing its own 24-hour emergency service. Moreover, Mercy is better equipped to handle serious life-or-death emergencies.

Specialty clinics are a third back-up service. As in most urban situations, the primary health care at HCHC is provided by internists and pediatricians. In addition the center has its own limited number of specialists—mostly on a part-time basis. However, specialized services are indeed restricted when compared to the range of specialties offered by top-quality teaching hospitals. For example, Mercy has 45 different specialty clinics, including chemotherapy, endocrine, infertility and endocrinology, and rectal. These specialty clinics make possible a level of care for HCHC patients available to only a small percentage of the nation's population. A continuing education function is also provided for the HCHC staff. Even though most do not have admitting privileges at Mercy many of them participate in the teaching and research functions of these specialty clinics.

The fourth back-up area might be called technological services. The most important are laboratory tests and x-rays. The x-ray service seems to provide a particularly crucial link between HCHC and Mercy and also involves the health department. Currently the center has no x-ray equipment of its own. In view of the size, sophistication, and quality of the project this is little short of phenomenal. The health department does have equipment in the building that can be used for chest plates. In recent years, however, they have not had sufficient resources to have a regular x-ray technician. The center has managed by using the health department's equipment. In return HCHC provides the personnel required to operate the machine and furnishes the health department with the x-rays they need. But today's medical care requires many other types of x-rays for proper diagnosis and treatment, and the center relies on Mercy for about 15 percent of total laboratory tests and x-rays.

There has long been unhappiness with this arrangement and subsequent attempts to work out something more satisfactory. But, as far as could be determined, little change has occurred since the opening of the center nearly five years earlier. The reason for this lack of progress is the shortage of space.

In summary the content of the linkage between Mercy and HCHC seems to involve primarily three factors: professional accreditation, fiscal responsibility, and back-up services. This last is particularly critical since it is based primarily on the center's need for specialized facilities, technology, and knowledge. Many of these activities could in principle be taken over by the center itself. There are, however, residual functions, for example, inpatient care and highly specialized tests, that cannot even in principle be shifted to HCHC—at least without transforming it into a very different kind of institution, namely, a teaching hospital.

External Linkages: OEO and HEW

A postscript is required about the network of interorganizational relationships discussed so far. During the first five years of the center's operation two links have been formally changed. First, the channeling of funds through the city's Neighborhood Development Office (NDO) was soon discontinued because that agency was rocked by newspaper reports of gross inefficiencies and subsequently stripped of many of its functions. Second and most important, federally funded health centers of this type were shifted from OEO to HEW. This seems to have had one rather immediate and possibly two longer term effects.

First, Mercy and HCHC experienced greater administrative difficulties with the new funding agency. Supposedly this is due to the more bureaucratic (or at least more cautious) approach of HEW personnel and to their inexperience in administering this type of program. When one of the Mercy administrators was asked what was involved in the transfer of funding from OEO to HEW, he replied:

Confusion. It may be just local problems or something, but HEW doesn't have the experience as of yet. They seem to be really trying though. . . . It's like suddenly they're saying, "How did we get you?"

This evaluation is supported by the comment of a person connected with the Southside Committee. When asked about the usefulness of interviewing the HEW project officer, she responded, "It will probably be a waste of your time; he doesn't know anything." Our subsequent interview with that officer largely confirmed the evaluation.

It is of interest that such an official would be chosen as liaison with a supposedly experimental program in an urban ghetto. The assignment of personnel is an organizational, not a personality problem. Of considerably more sociological and social significance than the particular personality involved is the disruptive effect of transferring a program from one agency to another. Clearly in this particular case there were short-term costs, but there were also longer term effects.

One was due to differences in OEO and HEW philosophy about who is the appropriate clientele or target group. In general OEO served primarily poor people. HEW, in contrast, wanted a mixture of wealthy, middle-class, and poor people. Supposedly this was to avoid segregating poor people and to make care more nearly uniform. But clearly HEW also wanted to reduce the amount of subsidies they provide to such centers. HEW pressured HCHC to increase the proportion of their patients who were covered by some type of insurance. But HEW offered little guidance about how upper- and middle-class patients, with resources to choose almost any health care facility they desired, were to be attracted to a crowded health center in a near-ghetto area.

The second, and related, change with possible long-term consequences had to do with funding. Centers like HCHC were planned on the assumption that a significant portion of their costs would be covered by Medicaid payments; OEO planned to cover operating costs in excess of the income from Medicaid. About two years after Medicaid was initiated the benefits available in the state were significantly reduced. This meant the cost to OEO rose significantly. When these centers were shifted to HEW this arrangement was changed. HEW simply pledged a specified amount of the total budget of each center. Moreover, they repeatedly warned the centers that the continuation of these grants was by no means certain. This threw the whole future of the program into question and to some extent lowered the morale and enthusiasm of nearly all the participants.

The shift of responsibility from OEO to HEW also significantly affected the relationship between the local institutions, especially the relationship between Mercy and HCHC. One got a definite impression that Mercy wanted to reduce their responsibility for the program as much as possible. The administrative ineptness of HEW and increasing uncertainty about future funding were undoubtedly important irritants. The inability of either OEO (or later HEW) to reach agreement with the city's health department certainly had very definite effects on the local linkages and made the resolution of several important local problems virtually impossible.

Secondary Linkages

HCHC has been viewed as a satellite of Mercy to emphasize the key interorganizational linkage and the dependency of the center on the founding hospital. But HCHC is not simply part of Mercy. It has a distinctive organizational identity and in many respects is an autonomous institution. Hence, HCHC has a series of secondary interorganizational relationships, that is, links developed in large measure on the basis of its own identity and program. One linkage has already been described in some detail: HCHC and the health department jointly use x-ray equipment. This is not a satellite relationship, of course, but two more or less equal agencies sharing equipment and staff. These two agencies also share dental equipment. The health department had a "terrible, very old-fashioned dental facility," reports a Mercy administrator. HCHC built "a very lovely new dental facility." The health department uses these facilities three afternoons a week, and the center uses them the remainder of the time.

As we have seen, the link between Mercy and HCHC has a number of dimensions. Now we see that HCHC has a secondary linkage to the health department, and it too has several dimensions: building space and sharing of x-ray and dental equipment. An interesting sidelight is how these dimensions interact on each other. To illustrate this, let us trace how this maze of multidimensional interorganizational relationships affects the efforts to secure new x-ray equipment. HCHC's work is hampered because it is dependent upon Mercy for x-ray services. The

needed x-ray equipment cannot be acquired, at least in part because the
health department refused to allot additional space to HCHC. One probable reason for this reluctance is Mercy-HCHC's never having signed a
contract for the space already occupied for the last five years. Mercy-
HCHC is unable to sign the contract with the health department because
their earlier contract with OEO (and subsequently HEW) gives that
agency veto power over contracts with third parties. HEW is unwilling
to approve the contract between Mercy-HCHC and the health department (or to allow actual purchase of the equipment) because federal
authorities and the health department cannot agree on who will own the
equipment (the already installed dental equipment and the anticipated
x-ray equipment) if HCHC should go out of business.

COMMUNITY PARTICIPATION:
THE SOUTHSIDE HEALTH COMMITTEE

As complex as the linkages described may seem, the most crucial and
problematic relationships have not yet been introduced: the attempt to
introduce community participation by linking the satellite health center
with a community council. To understand the nature of conflict and
neutralization in the Southside health care system it is necessary to describe in some detail the nature and dynamics of these relationships.

In our context community participation implies a mixture of decision-
making by centralized authority structures and by more "democratic"
symmetrical forms of interaction. This mixture of decision-making
mechanisms is, in part, an attempt both to obtain the efficiency of bureaucratic structures and to increase the degree of equality and communication between officials and clients (that is, "the community").

The concrete form this mixed structure takes is a linkage between the
professional bureaucracy of Mercy Hospital and the Southside Health
Committee. The committee is in part advisory and in part a board of
directors for the Heightsville Community Health Center. As we shall
see, the degree to which decisions are to be made by common bureaucratic means or by discussion and consensus formation (that is, interaction) is ambiguous and debatable. In any case the result is considerable
social conflict. This section describes the form and nature of this con-

flict. Special attention is devoted to the role of individuals who occupy key boundary positions. Also implicit in the description is a crucial subcultural difference in norms and values. Middle-class officials emphasize the importance of universalistic criteria, while members of lower class ghetto communities often have more particularistic commitments.

Dr. Warren and the Formation of the Committee

The OEO guidelines for community health centers required that the grantee, in this case Mercy, organize a community council to participate in the development and operation of the center. The Southside Health Committee (SHC) was formed pursuant to these guidelines. Soon two things became apparent. First, SHC was much more of a mechanism for regulating interorganizational relationships and gaining legitimacy with OEO than a representative body of either community members or potential patients. Each official member was a representative of some other neighborhood organization. Put another way, the "community committee" was formed largely by professional or semiprofessional community workers whose interests converged with the interest of Mercy, or more specifically, of Dr. Warren. According to one of the original members of the committee: "We were all self-appointed. There was money in Washington. You could get the money if you had both a back-up hospital and a community group. Mercy was interested and those of us in the community that knew about it were interested and we got together." Secondly, formal membership and participation was quite open and fluid, if not erratic, during the early months. As we shall see, this has continued to be a problem.

From the beginning there was disagreement over the committee's power and authority. A key Mercy administrator stated: "If you really read the vague, vague statutes or the vague, vague guidelines set up by OEO and HEW, no matter how you cut it, it's [the Southside Committee] advisory—with some specific advisory functions." However, according to a committee staff person SHC had from the very beginning sought the right to approve all hiring and firing. With such differences in perspective the more or less continuous conflict between Mercy and the committee was almost inevitable.

Perhaps the most persistent and intense conflict has centered around the project director. During the less than five years of HCHC's existence there have been two "regular" project directors and an interim director who has been in charge of the program for six months. Both previous directors were for all practical purposes forced to resign because of irreconcilable conflicts with the committee.

To clarify the nature of the endemic conflict surrounding the director let us look at some of the details. Dr. Warren was closely identified with Mercy. He was both an assistant director of the hospital, and therefore a member of the administration, and a physician who was a member of the medical board. As indicated earlier his community health department had many irons in the fire at Mercy besides HCHC. Exactly what forced him to resign is unclear. Purportedly a combination of many factors was involved, especially disagreement over the committee's role in setting personnel policy and hiring employees. Whatever the exact reasons, he resigned from both HCHC and Mercy and left the city and state.

Michael Baine and Jane O'Shea

In contrast to Dr. Warren, his successor, Mr. Michael Baine, was supposedly a "community person." He had been the executive director of Ricker's Hill Neighborhood Association, probably the most powerful organization represented on the committee. He was specifically put forth as a "community" nominee. According to his own account he had no past training or experience in the health field. Because of this, OEO delayed his appointment and was not persuaded to acquiesce until a group from the committee, the hospital, and the community went to Washington and sat in at the OEO office, demanding approval of his appointment.

The story of Mr. Baine's rise and fall is long and complicated. Since it is largely one of conflict and the observers were participants, there are no nonpartisan accounts. Our primary concern is with the relatively undisputed facts. Consequently, let us have one of the key participants tell the story, for she can do it more vividly than any attempt at a composite "objective" description. What follows is largely the account of Miss Jane O'Shea, who was Mr. Baine's chief assistant during most of his tenure in office.

There are many stories and I don't know if the real story can ever be known. This is my version.

Over a year ago he fired his secretary, Thelma Smith, a black girl from the neighborhood. Then because the secretary was a day late in applying for a hearing they wouldn't give the secretary the hearing. The council [Southside Health Committee] was supporting Michael Baine all the way. He brought pressure on them. He alluded to many things which were never made clear—alluded to possible indiscretions.

The secretary had a lot of friends and she said it was a racial thing. I don't think it was. I know it wasn't racial. . . . Friends and neighbors of the secretary got together and came to council meetings. Mike avoided four out of the next five council meetings. . . . He found convenient reason, always good reasons. . . .

As a result, a lot of the anger centered on Mike. So they picketed, and said they were going to go to picket Mercy later on in the week but they changed their minds. . . . the word was out that they were going to come into the center. It is not formal but at the same time it's a very strong grapevine. Everybody knew that they were coming up to confront us to see about Thelma.

When the demonstrators arrived at the center they saw Mr. Baine "going out the back door." A spontaneous and relatively good-natured sit-in developed.

It turned out to be sit-in for about a day and a half. Michael finally came at 2 o'clock in the morning. He played stupid like he didn't know there was a sit-in. Michael wouldn't come in without police guards. He claimed he was going to be attacked. That was . . . never real; it was always in his mind, always. Anyway, they yelled at him for an hour and a half, that's about it. Nothing was happening.

By complaining to Mercy and OEO in Washington, Thelma Smith did succeed in forcing the council to grant her a hearing, but Mr. Baine's decision to dismiss her was upheld—though the vote was close. These events led to a significant shift in Mr. Baine's status within the neighborhood community.

At that point the council began to wonder what's going on. Michael had been their friend. They had hired Michael; he was a community person. So then what happened was that the council and the community became a "little bit" disenchanted with him. They demanded Michael's resignation and a series of points. Mercy was shocked; it was the first they knew that there was any problem at all between the community and Michael.

In response to the committee's complaints, Mercy put Mr. Baine on probation for three months beginning in July. The next crisis developed over preparation of the budget.

Our budget year is up at the end of October. Michael had been very late the year before with that budget and the council had been after him for the budget. He asked all of the departments to submit requests to him by June 15th—a report for all the things we would like to have. That was a big budget—3 or 4 million dollars. It was what we would need to run an ideal center. It was just a line and a figure. But . . . that is not a budget. You've got to justify; you have to explain; lay out your program goals, your hopes, your dreams, whatever. That was never done. The council rejected it, turned it back to him and said it was insufficient. He said that he was waiting for more direction from the council.

During the summer the council [Southside Health Committee] worked with two outside activist consultants. They accused Mercy of "ripping off the program," that is, of inflating the cost of services provided to HCHC by the hospital's other divisions and charging these against the federal grant. In addition these consultants helped the council develop another proposed budget independent of the one submitted by Michael Baine. The new proposed budget included approximately $160,000 (more than a fivefold increase) for council expenses per se—as contrasted with operating expenses of the health center. The increased funds were to be used to train the council to take full responsibility for the operation of HCHC; federal funds would be channeled directly through SHC rather than through Mercy. Mercy claimed to share this goal, but they thought the request "excessive" and rejected the budget. There was a stalemate. The conflict between Mercy and the council made it possible for Michael Baine to counterattack.

Michael knew that he had to save his job. Dick Vroom is a community activist and a very close friend of Baine's. Of course as far as most people are concerned, they don't know each other. I know for a fact that they were close friends. Dick came to the October council meeting and a couple of days later Dick and the top staff people, Michael's clique, put out a call for the community to reconstitute the health council or some such thing. That was the beginning of the People's Health Council. Michael wasn't present at any of the . . . public meetings. He was present only at private meetings. . . . Dick and an old friend of Michael's from Ricker's Hill began to attack the committee and the consultants as "poverty pimps." Then they said the committee was not representative . . . nothing but a clique of people trying to take over the program . . . so you have this new group in the scene and they are attacking the council and the council is trying to fight back and meanwhile there is no budget. . . .

It became increasingly apparent that if the disputes over the budget were not resolved the entire HCHC program would be terminated by

HEW. This realization finally produced a compromise; the council and Mercy signed a formal agreement—called the Four-Party Agreement— that called for reorganization and arbitration in the event of further conflict.[2] The council also reduced its budget demands to $35,000. Although the compromise resolved some of the past conflicts, new ones soon emerged.

Then there was one other incident that should be mentioned; it shows you how everybody operates. There was a doctor who had been having trouble with a lot of people, and the medical director fired the doctor. There were charges like the doctor was fired because he was Puerto Rican, and the committee was hearing the grievance on technical grounds: not one procedure had been followed in the firing of the doctor. Therefore, he was automatically reinstated. While the committee was in the process of hearing the grievance, the People's Health Council came marching into the center and sat in to get this doctor back his job. Vroom said, "We the People's Health Council did it."

In the middle of February Michael Baine resigned effective the middle of March. Miss O'Shea comments on some of the interpretations of this event:

The stories are: either one, he resigned because he got tired and number two, he resigned because there was a deal made between the committee and Mercy saying that once everything quieted down, they would get rid of him. Who knows? I don't know. And the third story is the story that has gotten the most publicity, and there is absolutely no foundation to it whatsoever. After Michael resigned, Dick Vroom came out with a flyer saying: "Program director fired as a result of pressure from the People's Health Council." I have copies of every piece of literature they've handed out, and in not one piece of literature have they ever demanded or said anything against Michael. Most people don't read all the flyers or even more important, they don't save them, and therefore, they don't know.

As a result of this long period of conflict and disruption many were interested in reorganizing the program in such a way as to avoid some of the past difficulties. Several different foci of the reorganization emerged. One concern was to ensure that the Southside Health Committee was representative of the community. Arrangements were eventually worked out to hold a community-wide election to select the members of the Southside Health Committee.

A second key issue was the specification of who had authority over what. The responsibility for hiring nonprofessional staff was a particularly crucial issue.

The position of staff is that community control isn't hiring, isn't being in control of every job. That's chaos, once you have a group of people hiring people for jobs they don't even understand necessarily. . . . hiring their friends, which is what happens, and that's okay, because there's got to be something in it for council people. I mean, you know, every board operates that way, whether it's a filthy rich board or a poor board.

Miss O'Shea's comments about this matter are in some respects inconsistent. On the one hand she is a "realist" who says it is all right for council members to hire their friends. On the other hand, she strongly advocates giving the responsibility for hiring to the director in order to prevent this. As we shall see, this ambivalence, a core ingredient of the conflicts over community control, is structural rather than personal.

A third aspect of the reorganization efforts was to prepare SHC and HCHC to become legally independent of Mercy, though of course they would still rely on the hospital for back-up services.

I think the problem will be finding out what HEW wants and doing it. You've got to show them you're fiscally responsible and you can handle it administratively, produce good medical accountability. There's got to be a formal contract . . . with Mercy which says well, you're the back-up hospital now and this is what you do and this is what we pay you. It's a lot of legal stuff. If you don't do that, you're not going to get the power.

In sum, Mr. Baine started out as a "community person"—or at least the members of the Southside Committee thought that he was—but he wound up being rejected by the members of the committee. The committee demonstrated and protested to get him hired and demonstrated and protested to get him fired. Only intervention by Mercy delayed his departure.

Miss O'Shea seems to have become a "community person." She was apparently working hard to help the committee develop the resources and skills needed to become the grantee and take over full control of the HCHC program. She was subject to fewer cross-pressures than Mr. Baine since her job gave her greater insulation from the demands of Mercy and the center's staff—something that must have been a problem for Mr. Baine. If Miss O'Shea's account is biased, it is primarily biased against Mr. Baine and in favor of the committee. She did not become the chief staff person of the committee, because they perceived her to be a strong supporter of Mr. Baine. Surely she should have been willing and able to work with the community over an extended period and make a contribution to the program's development. Unfortunately such optimism was unwarranted. About two months after Miss O'Shea was interviewed she resigned her position and left the HCHC program entirely.

We have then the account of three people who have been unable to span the boundary between the community committee and the HCHC program. The first was Dr. Warren, who was highly qualified in medicine and public health, a proven administrator, and an organizational entrepreneur. Next was Mr. Baine, a person with significant experience in local community and organizational politics, someone with the strong backing of powerful elements within the local interorganizational and community structure. Finally, there was Miss O'Shea. She was apparently equally knowledgeable and astute about local politics but seemed more open and forthright in her dealings with all the parties involved. Yet, ultimately, each one proved to be unable or unwilling to work with the community committee for any extended period.

The problem may still be a matter of not having the right type of people to work with the committee. Significantly, all three of the individuals were upper or middle class in their life styles and perspectives. One was a physician and two were professional poverty workers. Perhaps the committee could get along with—and be effectively led by—someone who was really from the ghetto community, someone who was personally and intimately acquainted with the life problems of the underprivileged. Mac Brown, the Chairman of the Committee, was such a person.

Mac Brown's Story

Mr. Brown's story is highly personal and involves many elements besides interorganizational relationships or even conflict over the HCHC program. Nonetheless, interorganizational links have played a vital role in his life—and vice versa. This is the story Mac Brown told:

Up until the last five years I've been pretty much living outside of the system. I was an ex-offender, with a broad criminal history and I also was an addict until four and a half years ago. I began to try to fit inside of the system, to change my life style by first becoming a consumer of methadone. As soon as I was stabilized at Washington Hospital, on methadone, I felt that there was something else needed.

For a while Mac Brown assisted one of the physicians at Washington Hospital in a drug addiction education program; they went on speaking tours in suburban communities, but after a few months this program was terminated.

About that time I met a guy by the name of George Roberts who came to the hospital. Mr. Roberts asked me where did I live and I told him and he said well you're right in my community so perhaps we can interest you in getting on an advisory board related to the community and the nature of it, that it was an anti-poverty program and the delegate agencies that this board governs because it was on the board of the Southside Community Corporation and the corporation itself was more or less the umbrella program for the delegate agencies. Roberts was a member of the board at that time, chairman of the personnel committee.

Mr. Brown then visited the agency and spoke with Juanita Torres.

She said that the OEO mandate is that the board must be represented by, I think, it is two-thirds of poor people and they were trying to establish this for some reason it was not being done so she felt that if she submitted my name as a poor . . . , this would motivate other people to join and being an ex-addict and somebody on methadone, she felt that it would be advantageous to the community. I found out that this would give me a basis for more growth inside the system and I joined the program committee and we began to do some really good work.

After I had sat on that board for about a month, I was approached to join a board of this delegate agency, a subsidiary agency of the Southside Community Committee. They needed help but I said to myself, "I don't know if I'm ready to take on all of this responsibility." So I went to the hospital and I talked it over with my doctor and he said, "Sure you're ready for it. You're about ready to take on anything."

A few months later Mr. Brown was asked to be on the Southside Health Committee. He was reluctant but was encouraged by Harry Simpson, director of the Pontiac Neighborhood Conservation Association:

I told him that I was already sitting on two boards. He said, "Yes I know. That's why I'm asking you because you're the first . . . the second ex-addict on methadone that I've talked to and is beginning to do something with their lives." They just welcomed me right in. And they said, "Why don't you try the personnel committee because they have grievances. They are screening people for jobs and what not, and we feel that this would be something just down your alley."

During that summer Mr. Brown was offered a staff job with the United Southside Committee. To accept the job he had to resign his position on the board of that agency. The prospect of increased responsibilities led to an important personal decision:

Well also about that time I went to Dr. Tortoni and told him that I would like to be detoxified from methadone and he said, "Do you have that strength?" And I said, "I'm attending enough board meetings and that now that I'm working I feel sure that I don't need anything at this point." He said that a lot of people slip back if they get angry or if they're not satisfied with something. And I said, "It is sort of a challenge and I would like to undertake it." So he said okay.

In the meantime Mr. Brown became an active leader in the demands for expanded treatment facilities for drug addicts. "During the summer I had to beg off from the Southside Health Committee meetings because there was sort of a crisis with the youth in Wattsbury using drugs." His account of this shows the sharp contrast between his style of leadership and that of Dr. Warren, Mr. Baine, or Miss O'Shea:

In the meantime the demonstration in Wattsbury grew fruitful. People talked about ripping off some place so that the kids could have some place to go—at least to be detoxified. And we felt that we could get some social service people to relate to their domestic needs if we could get them clean. So the night after the demonstration we went to Wattsbury Hospital, the old building. We kicked open two doors in two different wards—about 12 o'clock at night. We had about 300 young people there laying on the floor and about another 200 older addicts there. We went out to the community and we begged cigarettes, we begged food. Finally the hospital responded because the community was up in arms. They eventually did get a grant and an ongoing program.

As his experience increased he became aware of some of the less idyllic aspects of community programs. The resignation of the chairperson of the Southside Health Committee was a particularly sobering incident. The agency she worked for tried to get her to support policies she was personally against. According to Mr. Brown, she resigned from the committee in an attempt to reduce the cross-pressures but despite this was subsequently fired from her job—purportedly for not supporting the interest of her agency while serving on the Southside Committee.

It was about that time that I began to read the history of the Southside Health Committee and the Heightsville Community Health Center. It was Ricker's Hill Neighborhood Association that brought this whole thing about—like they did Urban Renewal. And that they are the ones that really had teeth into the people

who were hired and most of the people that were hired at the time came out of
the Queensborough Health Council. And I said, "Wow! What is going on here."
And then . . . I began to look at the representation of the board. It was almost
the same but it was just opposite ethnically than what the Southside Community
Corporation was. I said, "Well, now, I am involved in Community politics!" I
say it [SHC] was controlled. It was nothing but a rubber stamp. I could see
that now . . . you know . . . sitting back. I felt that Ricker's Hill was somehow playing a part in controlling it along with the HCHC program director,
Mr. Baine, who previously had worked with Ricker's Hill.

With his new, more realistic perspective he became even more active
on the committee—and probably more effective. About two months
after the resignation of the previous chairperson, the committee held its
regular election for officers. Mr. Brown was overwhelmingly elected
chairperson. Shortly thereafter trouble and conflict within the committee
and the HCHC program began to surface. Mac Brown recounted the
conflicts over the firing of Thelma Smith, Mr. Baine's secretary. After
this he became increasingly concerned about Mr. Baine's covert influence on the committee. Very shortly other conflicts developed. The family health coordinators, nonprofessional employees drawn from the community, were required to take an extensive training program. But they
did not receive a high school equivalency certificate or any other kind of
credential. According to Mr. Brown, "If they left there and went to
another job, they didn't have anything to show for it; their grievance was
very real." Mr. Baine was opposed to granting high school equivalency
certificates—supposedly because he wanted to discourage people from
moving to other jobs as soon as they had completed the training program. As a result of what he considered to be Mr. Baine's undue influence, Mr. Brown began to use his powers as chairperson to reorganize
the committee:

So then I began to start to change the structure of the executive committee. I had
read in the parliamentary procedures that the chairman had the right to pick the
chairmen of committees and he could change any of these except the elected officials. What I did was ask for everybody's resignation on the executive committee. I brought in . . . certain key people that were knowledgeable about programs.

These conflicts eventually resulted in a complete rupture between Mr.
Baine and the committee:

We set up a set of grievances and charges against him. At that time they—
Mercy—told us that we couldn't fire him because we didn't pay his salary; that
the best we could do was put him on probation for 90 days and then if he didn't
work out we could then . . . come back to Mercy with a recommendation that
he be fired and then, together jointly, we would deal with him. In dealing with
Mercy, we went through trying times when we found out that the council wasn't
anything but a rubber stamp.

Finally, they filed a law suit against the hospital and Mr. Baine.

Mr. Brown then recounts how a compromise agreement was worked
out between the committee and the officials at Mercy: "We had to do
some kind of action to bring Mercy at least to feel that they had to
reckon with [the] community." Apparently the committee members were
not completely clear about some of the details of the agreement but had
one overriding concern: ". . . that the grantee [that is, Mercy] shall
move diligently to prepare the board [Southside Health Committee]
. . . to become the grantee of the program." Yet Mr. Brown had anxieties
about the committee's ability to operate HCHC completely on their own.

We had workshops . . . on the health center and how they were funded and the
language that OEO wrote and it seemed to me that we were going to need more
than just this training if we were ever going to become the grantee. We had to be
thoroughly trained in management and budget proposal writing and narratives
and work programs and the whole thing. I didn't know that stuff. It frightens me
to think that if the hospital had said okay and HEW had agreed so you can
become the grantee and just give us a whole chunk of money and says go ahead
about your business . . . we wouldn't have known what to do with it and that is
a lot of responsibility. We wasn't ready for it and I don't know when we will be
ready for it. I have to be honest about it.

By almost any standards Mac Brown has undergone an amazing transformation and has made an important contribution to the stability and
effectiveness of the committee. But neither Mr. Brown's position of influence nor the policies and concerns he supported were secure for the
long run. In the community election a few months later, a month after
our field work was terminated, Mac Brown was not reelected to the
Southside Health Committee.

Chapter Nine

NEUTRALIZATION AND CONFLICT

In this chapter the data relevant to neutralization and conflict is brought together and analyzed. Before this can be done, however, these concepts must be more clearly defined. First, keep in mind that up to now the analysis has focused on the integration of activity. Integration is synonymous with the concept of coordination except that the latter term usually implies conscious decision-making and deliberate actions. The term *integration* has been used to make clear that activities can be fit together by means other than conscious and deliberate effort. Coordination is one means of integrating instrumental activities. Moreover, the integration of activity does not necessarily imply anything about the integration of sentiments, ends, or values. Value consensus is one means of integrating instrumental activity, but various forms of pressure, coercion, and compulsion are other common means.

With this in mind let us turn to the concept of conflict. For our purposes we must distinguish between two levels of conflict. The first implies that things do not fit together, as when we talk about a scheduling conflict. On this level, conflict means that two sets of activities are incompatible; one set gets in the way of the other. Often this type of conflict is due to scarcity; we cannot build tanks and cars with the same steel or have a parade and fast-moving commuter traffic on the same street at the same time. Let us recall two examples from our data. The efforts of HCHC to provide comprehensive health care at the Southside Health Center conflict with the need of Mercy for specialized outpatient clinics for research and training purposes. Second, the desire of the members of the Southside Health Committee to appoint nonprofessional staff conflicts with the administrative staff's desire to control these appointments. Conflict on this level by definition reduces the integration of activities, because the accomplishment of desired goals of at least some of the actors is reduced: research, teaching, and comprehensive care are all desirable ends, but in some ways they interfere with one another. Conflict on this level need not involve social interaction between the actors who are getting in each other's way. Actors can be unaware of each other and of the fact that they interfere with each other's activity, though such ignorance is undoubtedly the exception rather than the rule. For lack of a better phrase I refer to this level of conflict as a *conflict of interests* or activity conflict. In contrast I refer to the second level of conflict as *social conflict*. According to Lewis Coser social conflict means that "the aims of the opponents are to neutralize, injure or eliminate their rivals."[1] Social conflict (in contrast to a conflict of interest) necessarily involves social interaction. More often than not it involves deliberate attempts by the parties to sanction the other negatively. Usually social conflict arises because there are serious conflicts of interest. But the important point is that the two types of conflict are sometimes very weakly related. Conflicts of interest often do not result in social conflict, and moreover, on occasion social conflict is not due to any significant conflict of interest. Most of what Coser calls unrealistic conflict is of this latter type;[2] scapegoating is the classic case.

Conflict of interest can, however, result in at least two possible outcomes other than social conflict. One is a sequence of interaction that rearranges and fits together the activities of the various actors so as to reduce conflicts of interest and increase joint activity. This is, of course, what we mean by integration and coordination. But there is a second possibility; the actors may engage in an extended sequence of interaction without significantly reducing the conflict of interest or resorting to aggressive social conflict. That is, the efforts of the various actors more or less counteract each other. I refer to this outcome as *neutralization:* there are high levels of interaction, but they lead neither to additional integrated joint activity nor to open social conflict.

This chapter analyzes why high levels of open social conflict have surrounded the Heightsville Community Health Center. Of particular interest is why the level of social conflict has been so much higher between

Mercy and HCHC than between Mercy and Johnson—especially when there would seem to be a greater conflict of interest between the latter pair.

PERSONALITY, POLITICS, AND STRUCTURE

First we need to reject as inadequate the typical "commonsense" explanations of neutralization and conflict. Obviously there are positive and negative aspects of HCHC's network of linkages. HCHC could not operate at all without the support of Mercy, the health department, OEO, and HEW. On the other hand the quality of the center's program apparently would be improved by less dependence on Mercy (especially for x-rays), greater coordination between OEO and HEW, and a less defensive and possessive attitude by both the city health department and HEW. Yet the shortcomings of the various agencies are evidently due primarily to contextual structural factors rather than to the immediate personalities involved or even simply the structure of relationships on the neighborhood level.

The data provided so far might suggest that a primary bottleneck is the pettiness and defensiveness of the city's health officer. Could not things be worked out if this official were more cooperative? Comments by the Mercy administrator having primary responsibility for the HCHC program are enlightening in this regard:

And we would like to put another bucky [x-ray] table down there. It's a question of just working this out with the local health officer, and she's really been great. I don't know what's going to happen when she leaves. . . .

The main bottlenecks seem to be vested professional interest and the sheer complexity of the health care system. The same Mercy administrator comments farther about one attempt to solve some of the problems:

. . . We made a proposition to the city that we could take on all of their functions that they give in this [district] building, and give patients comprehensive care, if the city would give us the total space. Sounds plausible?

We got so hung up on unions. You know there's a doctor's union that works for the health department. They had a fit. The local city union of nurses and clerical staff saw this as the voluntary system taking over the city system. They declared that if we did this, they would pull all the city workers out from the whole city. All of this over our proposal.

Whatever the merits or demerits of the proposal, this shows the extreme difficulty of accomplishing relatively small changes on even a local neighborhood scale. The structural complexity and interrelatedness of urban health care systems and the vested interests in these existing structures make change difficult even when the two agencies primarily involved can agree on a course of action. Mercy's difficulty in implementing the new ambulance system suggests the same conclusion.

A second related point should be emphasized; to understand local linkages we must look at them in the context of superordinate links. We have seen two examples of how changes or problems at the superordinate level affect local linkages: the shift of federal funding from OEO to HEW and the inability of the federal funding agency and the city health department to agree on who would own equipment if HCHC went out of existence. Petty politics, lack of cooperation, and empire building are not difficult to find in local-level interorganizational relations. But often we fail to see that such behavior is encouraged if not produced by structural pressures and constraints from above.

INNOVATION AND COMPLEXITY

In an important study of interorganizational relations Herman Turk found it was easier to introduce poverty programs into cities having well-developed, relatively complex organizational networks.[3] Generally innovation studies have found that complexity and cosmopolitanism increase the likelihood of innovations. While this conclusion is probably true it can be misleading. Just because new programs are introduced does not mean significant changes occur in either the level of services or the distribution of power and privilege. The same complexity allowing the introduction of new programs may also play a crucial role in preventing them from having a significant effect. Our data show it is possible to suggest, discuss, and apparently come close to introducing an innovation without actually completing the process. Mercy's attempt to reorganize the ambulance system and HCHC's efforts to secure their own x-ray equipment are good examples. This parallels the critique of intellectual freedom under pluralism: nearly anything can be put on the agenda, but the probability of radical ideas' being taken seriously, much less affecting

behavior patterns, is very low.[4] My point is not that other political arrangements are superior with respect to intellectual freedom. Rather I
want to consider the implications of the critique of pluralism raised to a
higher level of abstraction and applied to the health sector. This procedure implies a model that would predict it is relatively easy to get proposed changes extensively discussed, and even accepted in principle, but
very hard to get them actualized. This is, of course, what we have
found, and it parallels the findings of Alford and Warren.

NEUTRALIZATION VERSUS COOPTATION
AND DIVERSION

Usually satellites are relatively new programs. More often than not,
however, they are created in the midst of a number of already existing
programs. Often the specific purpose of a satellite is a task that the existing organizations seem to be incapable of doing. The creation of such
satellites is usually an implicit admission of the ineffectiveness of existing
organizations. Unsurprisingly the established organizations are often sus-
picious if not hostile to the new intruder. Despite the fact that the new
organization may be intended to overcome the limitations of the existing
institutions, it will nonetheless have to come to terms with them. As
Philip Selznick found in his classic study of the TVA, one of the common means of doing this is cooptation: taking into the new organization
representatives of groups whose support is needed for the new organization to carry out its work.[5] When new organizations devote extensive
time and energies to working out cooperative relationships and "coordinating" their efforts with existing organizations, this often involves
some degree of cooptation—attempting to gain the acceptance if not the
support of powerful actors in the environment. Certainly HCHC's relationship to the city's health department must be seen in this light.

   One common outcome of the cooptation process, according to Selznick, is that the original goals and aims of the agency are often subverted
and watered down in order to reach a tolerable compromise with en-
trenched local actors. He claims this is what happened when the TVA
worked out relationships with established agricultural interests and the
land grant college system. Selznick's analysis points to the danger of a

sell-out—the original goals being abandoned, subverted, or transformed to suit the interests of established groups.

A second outcome might be called diversion. The notion is that those interested in reform are allowed to introduce incremental reforms as long as it is reasonably certain they will produce no significant changes. While the principle of reform is publicly accepted, enormous levels of energy are required to produce even modest changes. A number of analysts have seen this as a more or less self-conscious means of preventing meaningful reform. Robert Alford comments with respect to efforts to introduce community participation:

Even if community groups are represented on planning committees for new facilities, one highly likely consequence is that their activities by themselves will block new programs and projects. Once community groups are mobilized, they tend to conflict with each other and with the professionals in health organizations over funding, priorities, timing, sites, and control. Community participation is a classic instance of the "veto group" process leading to stalemate. . . . Such a typical pattern is no accident.[6]

Speaking more generally about urban reform Roland Warren says:

. . . it is difficult to see how serious innovation can arise from strategies that accept the existing institutionalized thought structure. Whence would they arise? And how would they escape the preventing-blunting-repelling sequence? It is equally apparent that the quest for innovation as it is pursued with and by these community decision organizations can be expected to confine itself to minor modifications in program, structure, and relationships which permit and support a continuation of essentially the same strategies based on the same analytical paradigm for understanding and responding to the social problems associated with poverty in the inner cities.[7]

In cooptation the reform efforts are diverted and transformed to serve the interests of established groups. In diversion reform efforts are led into blind alleys and dissipated.

But a third potential outcome is illustrated by the experience of HCHC. In situations with many organizational actors a more common outcome may be for interorganizational relationships to become so complex that neutralization and inaction result—rather than cooptation or conscious diversion. HCHC's experience in trying to secure additional x-ray equipment is a good example of such an outcome. No one explicitly opposes HCHC's having the additional equipment; in fact all would probably acknowledge that such a step is needed and worthwhile. However, so many actors are involved and so many interrelated decisions are required that it has been impossible to reach the needed consensus on all the issues. This leads to a set of propositions that are obvious theoretically but are often overlooked in the design of actual organizational networks in the welfare sector: the larger the number of actors, the more complex the decision-making process is likely to be because the larger the number of interrelated decisions required. The larger the number of such interrelated decisions required, the lesser the probability of achieving a consensus about each of the needed decisions. Consequently, the probability is greater that a standoff will result, neutralizing the interests and influence of the various actors. The result is inaction rather than cooptation or diversion.

In empirical situations the distinctions among cooptation, diversion, and neutralization are not always clear cut. Nonetheless the conceptual distinctions are worth maintaining. The first two concepts imply that those involved in the immediate situation more or less consciously subvert reform efforts—in the first case by a takeover and in the second by guiding reforms into blind alleys. Neutralization on the other hand does not necessarily imply conscious intent. It can result simply from ignorance or ineptness of the actors. If intent is involved it comes to play in the creation and maintenance of more general levels of social organization, for example, in legislation or ideologies governing interorganizational relations in general. Stated another way the institutional context channelizes and shapes activities so that the outcome is neutralization—whatever the intent of the specific actors involved in the immediate situation. Roland Warren has made a similar argument, using the concept of "institutionalized thought structure."[8] I have tried to give approximately the same notion slightly more specification by contrasting the almost unconscious effects of institutional context on neutralization with the more conspiratorial notions of cooptation and diversion.

In this case the context of the institutionalized thought structure is the ideology of coordination. This ideology encourages more complex relationships, but the absence of well-established simplification mechanisms makes actual achievement of integration difficult, if not impossible. Ironically, the ideology of coordination may in some cases actually reduce the level of productivity. The ideology exhorts organizational actors to expand the array of activities they attempt to coordinate with other organizations. But the simplification mechanisms needed to resolve the complexities and conflicts that arise are often unavailable; the net result may be to increase the ratio of interaction to activity without increasing the integration of activity. More time is spent talking and arguing about how to coordinate the various organizational efforts, but little is ever resolved. In this context talk is not cheap.

MANDATED DIFFUSE LINKAGES

Unlike the linkages Johnson Hospital formed with Mercy and other high-status institutions, the link between Mercy and HCHC is primarily an involuntary mandated relationship. The satellite relationship legally binds the two parties together, at least over the short run. Disagreements focus on the terms of the relationship; discontinuing the relationship because of lack of agreement is not a live option. Consequently when Mercy's and HCHC's interests conflict there is a much higher probability of open social conflict since the two parties must continue to interact on some terms.

Moreover, the expectations for mandated diffuse links are necessarily different than for voluntary relationships. Legally speaking Mercy owes Johnson nothing. In contrast it is legally responsible for the proper operation of HCHC. Mercy receives large amounts of money from the federal government specifically designated for the operation of that program. Consequently both the staff and the Southside Health Committee are very concerned that this money be fully used for the benefit of this specific program and not for the general benefit of Mercy. On the other hand, since the hospital is legally responsible for the operation of the program it must be quite concerned about the details of the committee's policy decisions and the staff's operational performance—much more than would ever be the case in voluntaristic relationships such as the one with Johnson.

The broad and diffuse scope of the relationship probably also contributes to tension and conflict. While for Johnson any one link is confined to a relatively few activities, the Mercy–HCHC link involves practically the full scope of the activities that make up the health center. Disagreements and tensions about one matter are easily carried over into other issues. For example, the disagreement between the Southside Committee and the hospital about the extent of the committee's authority seems to have spilled over into a budget fight. In short, when interorganizational relationships are mandated, broad conflicts of interest increase, hostilities intensify, and the probabilities of open social conflict increase.

These observations in some respects support and in some respects depart from previous findings. Hall and his associates found that a formal agreement or legally mandated relationship accentuated the negative correlation between conflict and coordination. This, of course, parallels our findings. But he also found that power differences were uncorrelated with coordination when relationships were formal or mandated. Hall concludes, "When the basis of interaction is mandated, the power issue is apparently resolved. . . . This is not to say that there are no power differences, but that these have apparently been accepted by the parties involved and are no longer an issue."[9]

Our findings in some respects suggest the opposite. In the informal voluntary relationships between Mercy and Johnson coordination would seem to be relatively high and conflict low. The reverse seems to be the case for the Mercy–HCHC relation. More specifically and accurately the problems occur between the HCHC administration and the Southside Committee. This suggests that the main difference between Hall's findings and our own have to do with the class and subcultural differences between the two organizations being linked. The links Hall studied appear to be primarily between bureaucracies populated by middle-class professionals. The Mercy–HCHC–Southside Committee link, however, links middle-class bureaucracies with a lower class quasi-political group. Now let us specify in greater detail the problems such links encounter.

CULTURAL CONFLICT: UNIVERSALISM AND
PARTICULARISM

In chapter 5 we found that universalism and particularism had an important effect on the likelihood that interorganizational links would develop. If the linkage involved the processing of standardized cases so that decisions could be made by relatively simple universalistic rules, no personal relationships were necessary. Transferring patients from an institution filled to capacity to a hospital with empty beds serves as an example of how such a social process operates. Where the matters requiring a decision were unstandardized or infrequent, and therefore not conducive to decisions by universalistic rules, particularistic interpersonal relations were usually a precondition for the development of an interorganizational link. In a sense universalistic rules could be substituted for previously established particularistic relationships and vice versa.

However, the choice between particularistic and universalistic criteria is affected by factors other than the uniformity and standardization of the cases or the existence of particularistic interpersonal relationships. Particularism and universalism can be general modes of orientation institutionalized on the cultural or subcultural level. This seems to be precisely the case with respect to differences between the "culture" of Mercy and that of Heightsville. There was a conflict on the level of sentiments, values, and general normative orientations used for decision-making. This produced a conflict of interest on the level of activities that in turn produced overt social conflict.

One form that this subcultural difference takes is the dilemma between the need for "responsible administration" and the need for "community participation." By responsible administration I refer to values such as punctuality, an appreciation of the utility of accurate records, planning, orderly procedures, "rational" analysis, and honesty (more specifically a clear separation between organizational resources and private resources). These values are not as prevalent among lower class minority communities as they are among the middle class and upper class, especially those elements of the middle class whose particular occupation makes them administrators or bureaucrats. This is not to imply that most members of the lower class are dishonest, disorganized, or irrational in any moralistic sense, but the two groups have different values and expectations. If the community committee is representative of the neighborhood, it is likely to slight these values in the eyes of middle-class administrators, in this case, the officials of Mercy and OEO–HEW.

NEPOTISM AND PARTICULARISM

The conflict over universal and particular criteria is especially clear in the handling of personnel matters. Some of Miss O'Shea's and Mr.

Brown's comments suggest nepotism has been a problem and that the committee's reluctance to give up the right to hire and fire involved more than a matter of principle. This is difficult to document, however, so let us restrict ourselves to specific incidents discussed in narratives presented.

First there is the appointment of Mr. Baine. He clearly did not have either the educational credentials or the professional experience normally required to direct a health center. To mention only one factor he had no previous experience or training in the health field. What he did have was the political support of the Southside Committee because he had particularistic relationships with certain key member organizations and because he was personally known by many people within the community. In large measure he was selected by particularistic criteria. Only after significant pressure from local groups did OEO agree to overlook Mr. Baine's lack of qualifications on their standard (universalistic) criteria.

Whether or not the reasons for the dismissal of Thelma Smith, Mr. Baine's secretary, were legitimate and justified is unclear. It is clear that the committee denied her a hearing on a trivial technicality, apparently in large measure owing to the particularistic relationship Mr. Baine had with some of the members and because he threatened to expose "certain irregularities," i.e., failure to conform to universalistic norms. Several members of the community came to Miss Smith's defense "because she was a friend," that is, because of their particularistic relationship to her. Other community groups then came to Mr. Baine's aid, and according to one report, the group supporting him was headed by "an old friend of his." Ultimately, Mercy had to step in and demand that the committee follow the standard procedures for handling personnel disputes. A similar incident involved a doctor on the center staff. Observers agree he had trouble relating to people, but certain procedures were required to dismiss him. These were ignored and he was summarily fired. Again Mercy stepped in and demanded the standard procedures be followed.

Particularism was also apparent in the formation of conflict groups. Mr. Baine's friends fought for his appointment. Mr. Baine's "clique" and an old friend fought against his dismissal. Thelma Smith's friends sat in and picketed in her behalf. In every reported case conflict groups formed primarily, not around an issue, per se, but around a personality. Once again this particularism should not be overstated; clearly universalistic issues were at stake too. Yet when one reads the accounts of the participants one is struck by the heavy emphasis on personalities.

The differences in universalistic and particularistic orientations are a matter of emphasis and degree. Yet many of the conflicts surely involved the failure of the committee to follow what Mercy considered to be standard procedures and universalistic norms.

SCARCITY, PARTICULARISM, AND "RESPONSIBLE" ADMINISTRATION

Let us carry the analysis a step further and identify the source of the strong emphasis on particularism among lower class activists. The motives for participation on community boards are, of course, mixed. Undoubtedly most members are vitally concerned about the needs of the community and how a particular program is attempting to meet these needs. But almost inevitably a second item is high on their agenda of concerns: jobs. One of the scarcest items in ghetto communities are jobs that (1) pay reasonably well, (2) are open to those with few credentials or experience, (3) are located close to the place of residence, and (4) are relatively permanent and secure. One of the most attractive features of local poverty programs is the prospect of such jobs. Those who participated in local boards were not necessarily seeking a job for themselves, but they were usually concerned about jobs for their friends and family.

One indication of how central the control of jobs is to the Southside Committee is the "Four-Party Agreement"—an agreement primarily between Mercy and the committee designed to resolve recurring conflicts. The document is four and a quarter pages long; two and a half of these deal with personnel procedures relevant primarily to hiring nonprofessional employees recruited from the neighborhood.

Poverty programs were one of the few channels of upward mobility open to those living in the ghetto, especially for older individuals finished with the formal education system. What is frequently not recognized is the necessary consequences this has for the administration and local politics of such a program. In probably every case the number of job opportunities made available by a program are much smaller than the demand. Hence, a very "selective" screening procedure is unavoidable.

It is hardly surprising that people who have low personal resources and who represent a community with few resources insist on maintaining control of this screening process.

Moreover, universalism is strongly related to affluence. Decision-making by universalistic criteria contributes to efficiency and justice for the average case but not necessarily for a specific case. The abstractions of universalism increase the percentage of the cases handled efficiently and fairly, but they may at the same time increase the chances of a specific case's being mishandled because the abstractions do not apply. Only where the actors have sufficient resources to "play the averages" is a universalistic decision-making structure appealing. Almost by definition urban ghettoes are communities with few resources where people manage to survive by virtue of particularistic social ties.[10] Community members tend, therefore, to rely on more particularistic criteria than the norms assumed by an administrating institution like Mercy.

Predictably these factors have a telling effect on satellite programs attempting to unite representatives from ghetto communities and rational–legal bureaucracies from an upper class and middle-class milieu. The same Mercy administrator, quoted earlier, comments:

The other problem . . . is, how can you expect in all honesty the community to be able to basically administer a program like this when so many of their day-to-day lives are so miserable? They can't even get up in the morning without having seventeen hundred things wrong, that you and I probably don't. . . . No heat in their house, being thrown out of their apartment, rats biting their kids, no food, and all the other problems of day-to-day living that they have. Now to expect that they are going to be able to turn that off and turn on policy setting for thousands of people is a very difficult thing.

Whether these comments are defined as condescending or insightful, the ghetto's pervasive and perpetual scarcity undoubtedly undermines attempts to involve community members in the administration of the program.

These findings are congruent with one of Benson's theoretical models.[11] Benson argues that ideological consensus, domain consensus, and work coordination vary together in an equilibrium but that ultimately they depend on resource acquisition. A difference in resources causes one subculture to emphasize universalism and the other to rely heavily on particularism. The difference in the emphasis on universalism and particularism indicates an absence of ideological consensus. This, in turn, is related to an aspect of domain consensus: the disagreement over who should have authority over hiring nonprofessional employees. These disagreements in turn reduce coordination and increase conflict.

BOUNDARY PERSONNEL

A concept of interorganizational conflict generated by the differing emphases on universalism and particularism provides a context for understanding both the role and the fate of key boundary personnel. In the previous chapter we looked at the attempts of four different individuals to span the relationship between the Southside Committee and the HCHC–Mercy program. These individuals ranged from a patrician physician to an ex-junkie. They occupied three different positions. Two of them were the director of the whole HCHC project (Dr. Warren and Mr. Baine); one was the chief staff person of the Southside Health Committee (Miss O'Shea); and one was the chairperson of that committee (Mr. Brown). Within two years after they took over their various positions—and sometimes sooner—they lost (or failed to gain) the support of either the committee itself or the members of the neighborhood who participated in the election of the committee, or they apparently lost interest in HCHC and took other jobs. Once again, perhaps HCHC has been unlucky and selected the wrong people for these jobs. But a much more likely explanation is that the built-in structural strains make meeting the responsibilities almost impossible or at least extremely difficult over the long run. Obviously these strains and contradictions are complex, but in large part they derive from the conflicting subcultural expectations regarding universalism and "responsible administration." The boundary personnel are caught in the middle of this cultural conflict. If they insist on universalistic values they run the risk of being labeled a "Mercy person" and losing the support of the committee. If they do not they can easily come into conflict with Mercy, the final power over their jobs and the HCHC finances. This is, of course, too simple a statement of the problem, but for the moment let us look at the career of Mac Brown in terms of this dilemma.

Mr. Brown is obviously a bright and articulate person with an above-average amount of dedication, openness, and candidness. He also projects a certain charming naiveté and, in the beginning of his career, a lack of political sophistication. Yet one gets the distinct impression that his mercurial rise to power and influence in Southside's poverty program is in no small measure due to his ascribed characteristics, as well as his charisma and abilities. What poverty and community development programs seek is not simply honest, dedicated, and talented people—in middle-class terms. Rather they seek people with these characteristics who also have attributes that identify them with the disadvantaged community. Mr. Brown is almost an ideal-type; not only is he bright, articulate, and honest, but he is black, an ex-addict, and an ex-convict. How "authentic" can you get? So we see Mac Brown being drawn, at some points almost pushed, into a maze of "community" programs. He himself soon plays a vital role in linking together a number of organizations. Like Dr. Mooreman, the Johnson–Bernstein chief of pediatrics, Brown is a clear example of the intrapersonal mechanism for linking together organizations through overlapping roles.

During the course of this story Brown describes his own concerns about nepotism, lack of administrative knowledge and experience, and the committee's ability to properly administer the program if they become the grantee. Yet for these programs to maintain their legitimacy with both local and funding groups, they must demonstrate this kind of "competence," plus significant community involvement, if not community control. What is needed are individuals who have certain behavioral characteristics of the dominant culture—punctuality, universalism (i.e., middle-class honesty), rationality, etc.—but who are also genuinely members of the community. Such individuals are rare, and most community boards seem to have a high percentage of either middle-class social workers or local politicians (broadly defined), who, by middle-class standards, are very low on universalism and overly blatant about their self-interest and nepotism. Consequently, people like Mac Brown are easily drawn into the center of things and almost fought over by the various organizations.

The Mr. Browns may not become central power figures. Probably more often they have relatively little real power and are constantly subjected to manipulation. At least that is what Mac Brown sees, "looking back on it." Rather such individuals serve primarily as key symbols of the two needed virtues: middle-class responsibility and lower class authenticity. They in some sense achieve within their personal characteristics the synthesis that is currently unobtainable in the form of social consensus. Group conflict is transformed into role conflict for the symbolic individual. This is not to suggest that symbolic solutions are not real solutions. But unless the underlying issues are eventually resolved they are seldom stable solutions. The issues were not successfully resolved during Mac Brown's tenure on the committee, and the symbolic solution provided by Mr. Brown's unique personality soon wore thin—and that particular symbol was discarded.[12]

A caveat is required that makes explicit the limitations of the analysis. Perhaps an analogy will help. People who drive automobiles with seriously defective brakes have a high probability of having an accident. The exact time, location, and circumstances of the accident are impossible to predict if all we know is that they have defective brakes. Moreover some drivers may be skillful or lucky enough to avoid an accident. If we wanted to understand the dynamics of each of the conflicts described or the exact circumstances causing the departure of the four individuals involved, the analysis would have to be considerably extended. But my purpose at this point is simply to identify the sociological analogue of defective brakes. Individuals who occupy boundary roles between rational-legal bureaucracies, to use Max Weber's term,[13] and lower class ghetto community groups are very likely to be involved in high levels of conflict and have high rates of turnover. Certain types of personalities, policies, and leadership styles may mitigate this. Rarely, however, can they eliminate the underlying strains rooted in the stratification system of American society and the differing subcultures it produces.

REASONS FOR PARTICIPATION

If satellite relationships almost necessarily involve high levels of conflict, why do the participants enter into such relationships? Why the lower class participates is rather obvious. Except for those with extremely high degrees of alienation or ideological fervor, something is usually considered better than nothing. Poverty programs offer "something"—at least some additional services and resources for the deprived community.

Why policies encouraging such relationships are promulgated and why well-to-do institutions such as Mercy participate in these relationships is less obvious.

One should not completely discount the hospital's genuine interest in improving the health care available to the disadvantaged. Fred Zarati, the Mercy administrator directly responsible for HCHC, states:

One of the things that he [Dr. John Warren] felt very strongly was the concept of establishing a free-standing, ambulatory-care center outside the hospital. He felt that he wanted to demonstrate that you could establish a comprehensive health care center for poor outside of a [traditional] health care institution. [He] felt that within the institution there were so many traditions and. . . . the largeness alone made it so difficult to change patterns of health care. . . . If anything we hoped this program would teach us rather than us teach them. We hoped that they would be able to bring something here that would show us a better way of delivering health to thousands of people.

Even if such statements cannot be taken at face value, there is no reason to assume that prestigious hospitals are in principle averse to helping the needy. As long as their basic established interests are not threatened they probably try to "do what they can."

We must not, however, assume that Mercy is "all heart." Perhaps they enter into such a hectic relationship because they are making money on the program. Under examination this proposition seems doubtful. As one of the HCHC staff comments:

Under HEW the money goes in a total figure to Mercy. They put the money in their left pocket and they pay themselves by putting it in their right pocket. Then they send you [HCHC] a bill after they've paid themselves. That was one of the many things they agreed to stop entirely. . . . Somebody could come in . . . and say, "Mercy is ripping off the community through this program." Well, you know my contention is, how much can you rip off a 2.4 million dollar program? We can add it up; we can figure that three hundred thousand dollars is about what they're creaming us for, one way or another. (A lot of it was for services, but I mean a lot of it.) But three hundred thousand dollars to Mercy ain't nothing. They're not just in this for ripping off three hundred thousand dollars. It's really a gross misstatement of facts that fits . . . ideological needs.

This statement seems to be a reasonable view of the situation. At the time of this study Mercy's total operating budget was nearly $40 million. It seems doubtful that a "profit" of considerably less than $300,000—probably less than half that much—is their primary reason for participating in this program given the administrative difficulties it created.

A third factor probably influencing Mercy's participation is the interest—self-interest, intellectual interest, and value commitments—of individuals and subgroups within the hospital staff. Some individuals, even within quite traditional institutions, are seriously interested in such matters as public health, health care organization, and improvement of services to the disadvantaged. A growing number of high-status professionals specialize in such matters, and Dr. Warren was such a person. He was a talented, energetic, and ambitious person "on his way up." As long as such individuals raise their own resources and as long as such programs are sufficiently insulated from the main programs of the hospital, the administration and the medical board probably will allow them to "do their own thing." Most of the existing satellite programs were initiated during Dr. Warren's term; few such programs have been undertaken since he left. This is not mere coincidence.

A fourth reason for Mercy's participation was to reduce the patient load in their emergency room and outpatient department. Shortly after Dr. Warren came to Mercy he conducted a study of the emergency room that indicated people were increasingly using it for routine health care. This was especially true of low-income patients. (This was due, at least in part, to the increasing scarcity of general practitioners—especially competent ones.) Moreover, the number of individuals treated by the outpatient department had for several years significantly increased. Both the emergency room and the outpatient department were overcrowded and inadequate for the demands placed upon them. After the establishment of HCHC, emergency room visits continued to increase, but visits to the OPD stabilized (see table 1). The HCHC program in part accounted for this stabilization. The Mercy administration probably anticipated this result. The comment of the hospital administrator quoted earlier concerning the effect of closing Johnson Hospital clearly shows that Mercy wanted to avoid an increase in their OPD load and was aware of how the services offered by other institutions would affect this. I am not suggesting that Mercy's participation in HCHC was simply a conspiracy to use federal funds to solve an existing organizational problem. But the prospect of reducing the patient load on the OPD was probably an element in the overall decision.

TABLE 1. *Indicators of Institutional Growth Patterns Over Eight-Year Period: Mercy Hospital*

Year	Employees	Inpatients Admitted	ER Visits	OPD Visits	HCHC Visits
8th	3,187	23,969	93,369	167,202	63,274
7th	3,359	22,883	92,229	167,122	53,048
6th	3,116	18,763	87,206	165,284	N.A.[a]
5th	2,976	20,459	86,289	169,136	N.A.
4th	2,971	20,459	81,501	159,977	
3rd	2,908	20,023	72,419	136,941	
2nd	2,568	20,223	68,325	149,045	
1st	2,667	21,053	64,657	147,426	
Percent Increase					
5th to 8th	+ 7.1	+17.2	+ 8.2	−1.1	
1st to 4th	+11.4	− 2.8	+26.1	+8.5	

[a] N.A. = not applicable.

A fifth factor might be the organizational prestige or empire-building syndrome. Other things being equal, the larger the program and the budget of an institution, the greater its prestige and the status of those who run it. This may have been a consideration in the decision to initiate the program, but any such enthusiasm for size seems to have waned. Several of the administrators specifically commented that a consensus was forming among the staff that Mercy was "big enough."

Finally, Mercy may participate in such ameliorative programs to avoid more drastic reforms in the health care system that might threaten its basic interests. This is related to the desire of nearly all organizations to avoid criticism and protest. These issues must be dealt with on at least three levels. The first is the neighborhood environment. Here Mercy seems to be making deliberate and conscious efforts to avoid criticism and conflict, no doubt in part because they have from time to time been the subject of protest demonstrations and on at least one occasion a four-day sit-in. Administrators frequently talk about their commitment to serve the local community. Michael George, Mercy's administrator, comments:

How we fill these goals—treatment, teaching, and research—has changed drastically in the last nine years [the length of time he had been associated with

Mercy]. All of a sudden we realized that we are not—we haven't been meeting the needs of the community. I think that up until five years ago we more or less thought of ourselves as a fine private institution rendering excellent care, but with no commitment to the people who live around the hospital center. This has changed—quite drastically.

This interview occurred about a year after the four-day sit-in. One does not have to be a cynic to suspect that the "sudden realization" was in part due to public protest against the hospital. On the other hand, most of Dr. Warren's community service programs were started before the most militant protests were experienced. Moreover, the hospital's response has not been entirely verbal. As a result of the sit-in the hospital agreed to open a 28-bed center for detoxification of adolescent drug addicts. In addition a full-time staff member has been appointed to deal specifically with community relations. According to Miss O'Shea's account, this step was taken after Mercy completely failed to anticipate the Southside Committee's demand for Mr. Baine's resignation. It is probably safe to say that Mercy is self-consciously trying to head off trouble on the local level and that attempts to improve health care for the poor, through programs such as HCHC, are related to these concerns.

The metropolitan area is the second relevant level. Several important coordinating agencies operate on this level: The Community Hospital Appeal, the Regional Health and Hospital Council, the Comprehensive Health Planning Agency, and the Regional Medical Program. Each has some influence over the distribution of governmental or philanthropic funds or over the approval of proposed changes in programs and facilities. Obviously institutions do not want to become labeled as "irresponsible," "encapsulated," or "unresponsive" by these important reference groups. A prestigious teaching hospital showing no concern about delivery of health care to the poor would quite likely lose status within this reference group. Hence, at least a weak relationship exists between these implicit pressures from above and Mercy's decision to participate in programs like HCHC. Such metropolitan area agencies are, however, hardly advocates of radical change. Token or symbolic programs are probably sufficient to maintain a member institution's good standing.

Finally there is the level of the national system. Do the staff, administration, and trustees of Mercy participate in programs like HCHC to prop up the existing medical system and class structure? In some senses they probably do, but it is unclear exactly how self-conscious this is. The majority of people we interviewed seemed to expect major changes to occur and either endorsed them or were reconciled to their inevitability. A comment by a member of the Mercy medical board illustrates this:

R: Well, I believe that each hospital center as a subdivision has proceeded to generate its own space, activities, ambiance, and so forth. . . . One of the problems is that it doesn't reach out in the community. It's only when the community gets into the medical center that medical care is offered. The Heightsville Community Health Center is one attempt to change this. I'm sure that in the future the situation will change strikingly. As I see it, the hospital will be given some funds by the city to render medical care for a certain area, to do it any way they want, and they'll find it would be much cheaper to deemphasize the bed unit basis of care and decentralize, and thus encourage, more community medicine.

I: Do you think your view of the direction things are going is generally held by other people on the medical board and is it viewed as positive or negative?

R: Most people, I think, tend to do what they've been doing last week and hope for the best.

In contrast, the medical director of HCHC thinks that Mercy is quite self-conscious and concerned about the public relations value of the center.

R: If we would pull out and say, "Mercy go jump in the river, we're going to relate to Washington Hospital," Mercy would hurt.

I: In what way?

R: Public opinion. I did not make this up. That's what they [Mercy] say.

I: I think that's right; public relations factors are not unimportant. Yet, it's not quite the same kind of day-to-day leverage. The fact that you depend on them for beds and you depend on them for x-rays and. . . .

R: They depend on the government for money and the government is dependent on votes.

I: O.K. In terms of the larger political context.

R: It's not negligible in the long run.

I: Can you talk about that a little bit more? How conscious do you think they are of this?

R: Depends on who you talk to. The administration knows it. Samuelson [Mercy's executive director] is no idealist as I read him. He knows it would be awful bad for Mercy if we pull out [in the eventuality that SHC becomes the direct recipient of subsequent HEW grants].

Whatever Mercy's original motives might have been for becoming involved in HCHC, their experience with the program definitely cooled and even soured their enthusiasm about such relationships. They seemed firmly committed to a tactful withdrawal that will minimize their connection with the program and the social conflict it involves. However enthusiastic health planners might be about reducing the inequities and duality of the existing system by linking high-quality, high-status institutions to institutions serving the poor, those who must enter into such relationships are at best reluctant. This is not primarily because these particular institutions or their personnel are any more callous or self-interested than other organizations and individuals in the society but because such satellite programs place these high-status institutions at a focal point of conflict. Like urban police, social workers, and schools, these hospitals become a primary and explicit point of contact between the haves and have-nots in our society. An interorganizational network based on an array of limited-purpose linkages characterized by symbiotic inequality (like the Mercy–Johnson link) in large measure allows high-status institutions to avoid this role and its responsibilities. Few institutions knowingly and willingly assume such a role.

PART IV

Chapter Ten

INTERORGANIZATIONAL INEQUALITY
IN THE WELFARE STATE

The essence of what I have described as a satellite relationship is to link two sets of social actors, each from a different subculture. One is the subculture of rational-legal bureaucracy with its strong emphasis on universalism and its close ties to other aspects of upper- and middle-class culture. The other group is from the subculture of poverty with its strong emphasis on coping via particularistic social relationships and is characteristically rooted in the lower class. These two are then linked in an ambiguous bastardized authority relationship with the joint responsibility for establishing an efficient rational-legal institution to serve (and eventually to be run by) the local lower-class community. As we have seen, conflict between these two groups is endemic and not infrequently epidemic. Moreover, the focus of the conflict is usually the hiring, firing, and promotion of nonprofessional personnel—both with respect to what norms will prevail and who will have the authority to make actual concrete decisions. In addition, the program is established as a "demonstration project" with no provision for long-term funding and virtually no possibility of self-sufficiency, given its commitment both to high-quality, comprehensive care and to serving the poorest members of the society. Even short-term funding depends on the representatives of the ghetto community being willing, in large measure, to adopt the universalistic norms of middle-class bureaucracies.

Offhand it might seem difficult to devise a surer formula for failure if one tried. But this is not the case. There are surer formulas. One is to give middle-class bureaucracies resources to serve the poor without making these institutions subject to even an advisory body representing those to be served. The result is usually an unresponsive and insensitive institution. Outpatient departments of most large urban hospitals are a good example. An alternative is to give funds directly to the lower-class community, or rather to an organization whose members are drawn from that community and who purport to represent it. Often the result is misuse of funds and what from a middle-class perspective is viewed as inefficiency. But if a satellite linkage is not the surest formula for failure, it certainly seems to be sure enough. Why is this approach to providing health care and other social services to the poor the best we have been able to devise? It is my thesis that the weaknesses of the satellite linkage are rooted in some of the basic cultural and structural features of American society. Let us now attempt to explore these contradictions.

ASSUMPTIONS ABOUT DISTRIBUTIVE JUSTICE

The strategy of satellites as a means of improving health care is in part rooted in commonly held ideological assumptions about what constitutes distributive justice. Of special relevance are the values of achievement and equality, and particularly the common cultural assumptions about the appropriate means of actualizing the latter.

Since its inception our society has valued individual performance and achievement. Our ideology, if not our actions, emphasizes that people should be rewarded, not on the basis of their inherited status or even according to their need, but in relationship to how much they have themselves achieved. At least in economic terms achievement is supposedly measured (and motivated) through competition in the marketplace. For the most part people's rewards, and therefore the goods and services they received, were supposed to be directly related to the importance of their collective contribution. Of course even at the height of laissez-faire ideology and free market competition, there were legitimate exceptions to this rule. The young, the sick or infirm, the old were not expected to earn their own way. Families were responsible for the care of incapacitated or inept members. A large family could by various means support several members who did not contribute to productive activities. Neighbors and religious and charitable groups were expected to assist when family units could not adequately shoulder the burden of the unproductive. In short, the "welfare function," the care of the nonproductive, was performed by families and other relatively local and particularistic social units, in the broader context of a reward system tied to individual achievement.

Though our ideology has stressed achievement, a strong emphasis has also been placed on the idea of equality. We in some sense believe that all people—at least white males—should be equal irrespective of their varying accomplishments. That is, rights and privileges are not legitimately linked to performance. All citizens are entitled to certain basic rights whatever their achievements or economic position. For example, all persons should have the right to vote, own property, and be tried by a jury of peers.

T. H. Marshall has argued that the history of equality in the modern world has been largely a matter of steady expansion of basic rights.[1] In the eighteenth century the focus was on civil rights: equality before the law and the courts, the right of all to hold property and participate equally in the marketplace, the right to enter the occupation of one's choice, and so forth. The emphasis in the nineteenth century was on political rights: the right to vote, to hold political office, to organize political parties, etc. In the twentieth century the focus has been on social and economic rights: the right to a basic level of education, the right to an adequate income in old age, the right to be protected against unemployment due to fluctuations in the business cycle, etc. Because of the society's tendency to define these amenities as basic human rights, the state has been called upon to develop programs to ensure that all citizens have these resources as a matter of right rather than privilege. These programs include public schools and eventually federal aid to education, social security, state and federal unemployment insurance, aid to dependent children, and other forms of "welfare."

In the last ten to twenty years the resource that has been the most redefined is health care. In the early 1950s the AMA was riding high, and to advocate "socialized medicine" was a sure sign that at best one was a Communist dupe, if not an outright card-carrying party member. In contrast we currently have AMA-approved government programs providing significant—even if inadequate—amounts of medical services for the old and the very poor. Eventually the federal government will, in all probability, ensure a minimum level of health care to all citizens. The current debate focuses primarily on what the minimum will be, what the form of financing and delivery will be, and when to begin. The Heightsville Community Health Center (HCHC) must be viewed in this context to see its larger significance. HCHC is one type of experimental program that is an aspect of the overall movement toward defining health care as a basic right.

This redefinition of basic rights, as a major aspect of the trend toward greater equality, is a form of cultural change, a redefinition of social expectations and to some extent a change in value orientations. Paralleling the cultural change, however, are some important structural changes. Most important, the relationship between the productive and the nonproductive members of society has been significantly changed.[2] The "welfare function," the support of the nonproductive, is less and less tied to particularistic relationships such as kinship or local communities. The increasing scope of basic rights of citizens is often not so much a matter of increasing equality as of shifting the welfare function to the state. As a result, the relationships between the productive and the nonproductive have increasingly been governed by universalistic norms and impersonal sentiments. The second important aspect of structural change has been a vast expansion in the significance of formal authority structures for governing these relationships. That is, vast government bureaucracies have been created and assigned the responsibilities of seeing that all citizens receive basic social amenities as a matter of right and of developing special programs that allocate government resources to those unable to secure these basic rights with their own resources. This threefold transformation—expansion of rights of citizenship, decline in welfare responsibility of particularistic units, and creation of vast welfare bureaucracies—is widely recognized, if not fully understood, as symbolized by the term "welfare state."

But there is an important qualification to the story of expanding basic rights and the creation of the welfare state. To a degree the emphasis has shifted from personal achievement to equality via the expansion of basic rights. Yet the value of achievement is still largely dominant. While it

may be acknowledged that all citizens have a right to basic levels of
health, education, housing, and the like, only those able to achieve these
things for themselves in the marketplace are looked upon as fully competent and responsible citizens. Those who must rely on the state to provide these basic needs are typically defined as inept or incompetent and
probably freeloaders. People may have the right to such basic amenities,
but unless they "earn" these for themselves (or inherit them from relatives) they in large measure forfeit their right to dignity and respect.

In short, while clearly the basic rights of citizenship have been en-
larged, the shift has involved considerable ambivalence, and the dominant cultural theme continues to be reward based on individual achievement. Consequently those who must rely on the government to actualize
their basic rights are typically seen as second-class citizens and more
often than not receive second-class service. It is in this context that the
organizational stratification of health institutions and the attempts to
reform them must be seen if their full implications are to be understood.
An ideology of coordination, with an absence of mechanisms to produce
it, contributes to the development of a stratified system of health institutions matching well our gut feelings about the type of service the poor
should receive. Such an arrangement means our society can give such
citizens the second-class service we privately feel they deserve while we
blame the inadequacies of these services on lack of coordination in the
delivery system. A corollary outcome is a self-fulfilling prophecy about
the ineptness of the public sector. Not unsurprisingly, when this sector
is given a difficult (if not impossible) task with limited resources and
fragmented power, the result is less than adequate. But then this outcome is attributed to the supposedly inherent inefficiencies of the public
sector and "big government"—and by implication reassures all right-
thinking people that virtue and efficiency are the prerogative of the private sector.

Another important feature of our ambivalent expansion of citizenship
rights is that our efforts at change focus on the poor. Reform is nearly
always formulated in terms of how the most disadvantaged can be
brought up to some minimum standard. Defining this or that service as a
basic right of citizenship is usually an attempt by the disadvantaged and
their liberal supporters to legitimate more governmental action on their

behalf. But this rationale for reform has an interesting corollary; it deflects discussion away from the privileges of the well-to-do. The social problem is defined in terms of poverty rather than inequality. This is true even when we focus on the interorganizational structure of the health care system. The problem was not defined primarily in terms of the excessive privilege and power of high-status hospitals but rather in terms of a need to create more nearly adequate special organizations to improve care to the poor.

So the implications of the total array of ideological assumptions are rather impressive. We support an image of altruism, solidarity, and concern for human need by formally expanding the basic rights of citizenship. But at the same time we focus the discussion on individual poverty rather than social inequality, reaffirm the legitimacy of achievement over equality, and stress the virtue of the private sector—all the while giving the underclass the inferior service we feel they deserve and blaming the inhumaneness of the outcome on the ineptness of the public sector and big government. All in all it is a most convenient and creative ideological formula.

Given this set of ideological assumptions and predispositions, it is understandable that an attempt to intervene in a pluralistic health system because of its increasingly stratified nature would almost inevitably take the form of creating a new publicly funded satellite organization to serve the underprivileged. Such a move matches well the traditional and dominant ideological assumptions.

COMMUNITY PARTICIPATION

But if satellite programs such as HCHC are steeped in relatively traditional ideological assumptions, some new elements are involved. Both clients and policymakers are frustrated with the inability of government programs to improve significantly the conditions of those they were intended to serve. There has been a special frustration with bureaucratic red tape and the unresponsiveness of officials to the legitimate concerns of the clients they "served." Typically most welfare efforts have followed this course: middle-class bureaucracies dispensed and lower class clients received. If the recipients did not like what they received or how it was dispensed they could in principle protest to elected political officials: members of Congress, legislatures, and city councils. But those with low income and status, taken as a total group, are unlikely to know who their elected officials are, much less attempt to communicate with them. Moreover, protest to elected officials has relatively little effect on the overall operations of government bureaucracies, though they may occasionally be effective in individual cases. Citizens needing help are too many, existing bureaucracies are too numerous, channels for communication are too long, and the procedures for protest through elected officials are too ponderous to have much effect on the day-to-day operations of these bureaucracies.

One attempted solution to this frustration was the addition of a new element to welfare bureacracies: community participation or, in its stronger version, community control.[3] This theme has strong precedents in American ideology. Beginning with the Articles of Confederation and the Constitution, the United States has had a strong bias against centralized governmental authority. Federalism, states' rights, decentralization, town meetings, and local control are all ideas expressing this more general theme. Therefore the notion of community participation not only offered a means of making bureaucracies more responsive to underprivileged clients but also did so in the context of a long-established and basically conservative tradition. The mechanism for making these bureaucracies more responsive is to shorten the lines of communication and authority between citizens and the local officials serving them. Community councils, committees, and boards are the primary organizational tools used to accomplish this. The lower levels of the welfare bureaucracies are no longer responsible only to the officials above them in the government hierarchy; they are also directly responsible to local community representatives. Of course, as we have seen, a critical issue is the nature and extent of the authority granted these community representatives. The commitment to community participation was at best ambivalent and ambiguous and was the source of a considerable conflict. It was based on the assumption that members of the underprivileged class could with reasonable ease become "responsibly" involved in the operational aspects of a complex organization on terms that would be tolerable for middle-class officials and politicians.

GOVERNMENTAL AND NONGOVERNMENTAL
ORGANIZATIONS

But a second new element was added. In addition to community control, attempts have been made to involve both private business and nonprofit voluntary agencies in the federal government's efforts to assist the poor. The role of Mercy is, of course, a clear example of this approach. Rather than directly establishing a branch institution of some federal agency, a grant was provided to a well-established high-status voluntary hospital. At least in part this mode of operation is another example of the increasing frustration with governmental bureaucracies, especially welfare bureaucracies. In contrast to the image of red tape and inefficiency that dogs most government bureaucracies, institutions like Mercy are seen as efficient, humane, and reasonably responsive to clients' needs. These are, of course, comparative statements; institutions like Mercy are often severely criticized. But when compared with, say, city or county hospitals, voluntary institutions usually come away with high marks.

At this point I must specify (and question) some of the implicit assumptions that lie behind the attempt to involve nongovernmental organizations. The greater efficiency and responsiveness of nongovernment institutions are usually attributed to two factors. The first is that they supposedly do not have a monopoly on the services they offer. If patients do not like Mercy they can go to some other hospital. In the past, if an old hospital was not meeting the needs of the local population, dissatisfied individuals and groups could found a new institution—though these possibilities have been reduced considerably by planning and coordinating agencies in recent years. In short, voluntary hospitals were supposedly more efficient and responsive because they had to compete for patients, while government-funded hospitals did not. The second factor is the absence of civil service security. Supposedly the less secure and more flexible reward systems of private and voluntary agencies encourage their employees to higher levels of performance and greater responsiveness to clients.

Perhaps these two factors have improved the performance, efficiency, and responsiveness of private and voluntary institutions relative to publicly supported institutions. But another critical difference between public and private institutions is frequently ignored: usually public institutions must, by law, serve all who have legitimate needs and apply for services. Moreover the population served by public institutions has a greater need for services and in many respects is more difficult to serve or treat. Those who form the lower class have greater medical needs;[4] even the rate and seriousness of mental illness tend to be higher.[5] A host of factors undoubtedly contribute to this, such as poorer diet, more crowded living conditions, and less preventive care.[6] The second point is more sensitive, but clearly, almost by definition, members of the lower class would find conforming to the expectations of middle-class professional personnel more difficult than members of the middle and upper class would. Once again a series of factors is involved, but lower levels of formal education are probably particularly critical. One need not assume that the norms and expectations of the middle-class professionals or the ability and willingness of middle-class clients to conform to these norms are in any objective sense superior to the "deviant" norms and behavior of lower class clients. But clearly the "deviance" of the latter group makes their treatment more difficult and expensive.[7] All of this is to make a very simple point: the greater efficiency and responsiveness of private and voluntary institutions are due as much to their dealing with a more selective clientele, who are easier to service and who contribute resources to the institution, as they are to any negative effects of government bureaucracy. The failure of private industry to demonstrate significant improvement in the operation of ghetto schools is highly indicative of this.

There is, of course, another reason to link new programs like HCHC to voluntary hospitals like Mercy, the need to coopt powerful actors in the new environment. Even if it were not assumed that nongovernmental institutions were more efficient there is great need to gain the cooperation or at least to neutralize the resistance of such institutions. In most local health systems the most powerful organizational actors are high-status voluntary hospitals. Hence organizing the reform efforts so that these actors perceive the new program as an opportunity rather than a threat is an astute move on the part of those who want to reduce the inequity of local health systems. However, Mercy's illusions about the benefits of such a relationship were soon dispelled. Mercy clearly wants out of the commitment to accept responsibility for this program aimed at the lower class. The problems revolving around community control are obviously a factor, as is the problem of a more difficult clientele. Even if turning the administration of such programs over to voluntary institutions would ensure an improvement in efficiency, this is not a workable strategy if our case is representative; the voluntary institutions are likely to withdraw from such programs once they have faced the difficulties involved.

A STRATEGY OF REFORM AND INTERORGANIZATIONAL INEQUALITY

This discussion has indicated some of the cultural and structural factors making a satellite health center a reasonable approach to reducing the inequities that had evolved in the Southside health system. There is no reason to assume either malice or stupidity on the part of those who conceived the program. They were undoubtedly genuinely committed to improving the health care of the poor. The program that developed was a reasonable attempt—given the ideological presuppositions common in our society. But just as clearly such a program at best will soften the harshest features of our health care system and leave the basic structure intact. Even these modest improvements will be limited to a small portion of the disadvantaged population. Such programs are part of a historic reformist pattern, not noted for changing core structures of economic and social inequality. Let us consider briefly some other examples of this traditional strategy.

As I have argued earlier, the common American approach to alleviating inequities is to create some special institution to provide services to the disadvantaged. This was the original purpose of hospitals; those not destitute were treated at home by private physicians. The educational system has gone through a long history of such programs. Governmental agencies have taken increasing responsibility for paying for longer and longer periods of education because the well-to-do have in part maintained their advantages by purchasing more schooling than the amount provided at public expense.

The most recent move in this direction has been the creation of a large number of community colleges. The avowed purpose is to provide higher education for those unable to afford more costly programs. But as the higher education system has expanded to include larger and larger numbers from disadvantaged groups, an increasing amount of interorganizational stratification has developed. The economically disadvantaged are very disproportionately overrepresented in community colleges and underrepresented in high-status universities. The benefits these different students receive are obviously unequal. The employment opportunities available to a graduate of a California community college (or even a state college) are significantly different than for graduates of the University of California at Berkeley. The life experiences of the high school graduate and the community college graduate are probably more similar than the experiences of the community college graduate and the Yale or Harvard graduate. Everybody receives more years of schooling, but the relative inequalities in life chances between the haves and have-nots remain largely unchanged.[8] There is the appearance of greater equity because new services are offered to the disadvantaged, but the old inequities are in large measure maintained by stratifying the organizations.

Another parallel is seen in the attempts at desegregation in the urban north. Public schools have by and large remained highly stratified because the middle class withdraws from those schools faced with the prospect of significant numbers of black students. This has happened not only at the individual school level; whole school systems have become predominantly black because of the "flight to the suburbs." Inequalities between individuals and groups are maintained by interorganizational stratification. More specifically the privileged are forced into a relationship with the underprivileged by some new law or regulation, but soon withdraw from this relationship by some means that is not regulated. The pattern of linkage, conflict, withdrawal exemplified by Mercy and HCHC is by no means a new sequence of events.

The parallel is perhaps even greater for mental health institutions. While considerable variation exists from state to state, public mental health institutions are usually overcrowded and understaffed. They provide little therapy and are often mainly institutions of incarceration rather than treatment. Populated primarily by those from lower class and lower-middle class origins, the institutions are rarely entered by individuals with financial resources. Members of more privileged groups rely on private counselors, psychiatrists, and private institutions that are expensive and exclusive. The extensive expansion of public mental health facilities during the 1960s modified some of the worst aspects of previous public facilities. However, the basic pattern of organizational stratification and consequent disparities in service and treatment was certainly not eliminated. It is debatable whether there are even significant changes in the pattern of inequality.

While admittedly many private institutions serve patients from a wide variety of socioeconomic and ethnic backgrounds, they are not usually required by law to serve all citizens within a given political jurisdiction. In large degree public institutions are subject to such a requirement. As we have seen, this usually has two consequences. Public institutions are not able to turn away clients when the demand threatens to reduce operating standards; to a significant extent private institutions can. This difference is a matter of degree and should not be overemphasized. Nonetheless, it is a significant factor. Secondly, and of even greater importance, is one of the effects of this inability to select and control the flow of clients: the facilities of public institutions tend to be more overtaxed than those of private institutions. Consequently—and here is the obvious but critical point—there is a tendency for those with sufficient personal resources to avoid public institutions. This in turn has at least two further ramifications. The first is that it greatly reduces the chances of the public institution's being able to charge their clients for any significant portion of the services provided. Affluent clients and patients do not normally go to public institutions; the facilities are overcrowded and the service or care is usually perceived as inferior—whether or not it is in fact. But a second and possibly even more significant result of this selectivity is that the public institutions end up with the clients who have greatest needs and are most difficult to serve.

PLURALISM AND INTERORGANIZATIONAL INEQUALITY

The pluralistic nature of the health care system is by no means the only source of the interorganizational stratification that occurs, but it does allow those with privileges to limit the effect of attempted reforms. In a unified system controlled by centralized authority, it is more difficult for different subunits to deviate publicly from rules and standards that supposedly apply to the whole system. Such deviations undoubtedly do occur, of course, but they are less easily justified and maintained over long periods. In contrast even agreed-to-norms and standards vary within a pluralistic system; each unit has considerably more autonomy from external control. Let me illustrate this hypothesis concretely. We would expect to find a narrower range of variation in norms and standards within the federal system of veterans' hospitals than we would between a set of hospitals related in a pluralistic system, for example, all the members of the hospital association in any large metropolitan city. Or we would expect to find a narrower range of variation between the different institutions in a state prison system than we would between city and county jails in the same state. Obviously variations occur in both systems where official norms call for such variation, but this is not the problem concerning us. No formal public policy says that the patients of low-status hospitals should receive inferior care and insensitive, impersonal treatment or that prisoners in the jail of city X should be treated humanely while those in the jail of city Y are regularly brutalized.

One reason the fight over racial inequality in schools is increasingly linked to variations between school districts is that legal action has made it more and more difficult to maintain schools of different quality or racial makeup within the same school district. Such districts constitute unified systems controlled by centralized authority. In contrast the public education system as a whole is highly pluralistic, being composed of about 18,000 "independent" school districts. Consequently as inequalities became untenable within lower level centralized systems they were often reimposed on the higher level pluralistic system. In education interorganizational stratification has tended to shift from the level of schools to the level of school districts—where pluralism still operates.

The recalcitrant interorganizational stratification observed in the Southside health care system and alluded to in the preceding discussion is certainly not a definitive general indictment of pluralist systems. We can, however, tentatively conclude that reducing inequities between health, education, and welfare delivery institutions is very difficult when such systems are highly pluralistic. When one form of the inequities is reduced or eliminated they often reappear in another guise.

THE WELFARE FUNCTION AND THE PRODUCTIVE FUNCTION

But lest it appear that the high-status institutions are the sole villain of the plot, the analysis must be carried a few steps further. As noted, the welfare function has been increasingly shifted from the family and other particularistic social units to the nation-state.[9] In the United States, however, this shift has at the most been partial. Even with private insurance, Medicaid and Medicare, millions of individuals do not have the resources to meet minimal medical needs. In a large degree our society simply allows these individuals to go without adequate medical care. But at the same time we have increasingly pressured welfare institutions such as voluntary hospitals to bear some of the financial burdens of the welfare function. That is, we have demanded they take on some patients for whom they will receive no financial reimbursement. Implicitly they are expected to make up these losses by charging higher fees to patients covered by insurance and other third-party schemes. This is parallel to the norms by which the traditional family doctor was supposed to operate: charge the well-to-do enough so that he could "afford" not to charge those unable to pay. Such an arrangement may work tolerably well when an individual or institution serves a community where the large majority can pay the health provider by one means or another and where the provider knows the clients well enough to determine their ability to pay. But as medical costs have risen and as urban areas have become increasingly segregated by race and socioeconomic status, it has become very difficult for hospitals to serve as the "taxing" agency extracting a sufficient "surplus" from the well-to-do to cover the cost of the welfare function. A 1974 study of Washington, D.C., hospitals indicated that 19 percent of the average daily charge of $170 went to "free and discount services, charity care, and bad debts."[10] In short, urban hospitals have been caught in the squeeze between the abdication of responsibility by traditional particularistic units and the refusal of the state to fully accept this responsibility. The result has been a process whereby some institutions were able to maintain their quality and prestige by sloughing off a disproportionate share of the welfare function onto lower status institutions in their immediate environment.

We must push the argument one more step even though it takes us beyond the data or even the health and welfare system and leads us into highly controversial issues. Why have traditional particularistic units—for example, kinship structures—"abdicated" their responsibility? First of all, many of these units have simply ceased to exist. The urban density and geographical mobility characterizing modern life simply leave no room for the lifelong primary groups that exercised much of the welfare function: the extended family, the church, the lodge, the small town. Modern life does, of course, include significant primary relationships, but for the most part they do not involve the networks of people with lifelong commitments and stability needed for such institutions to carry out the economic burdens of the welfare function. Secondly, those primary groups that do maintain relatively long-term relationships cannot function adequately in our economic system if they have the primary responsibility for meeting the needs of the nonproductive. The family unit that must carry the primary responsibilities—financial, social, and psychological—of meeting the needs of its sick, aged, and incapacitated members is, on the average, in a poor competitive position within the labor markets of our economy. The young business executive who must limit his geographical mobility and his business-related social life because of an infirm mother or mentally ill sister is less likely to make his way up the corporate ladder than someone who does not have these responsibilities. The unburdened individual in all likelihood devotes more of his energies to company business and is more economically productive. Moreover, a whole economy made up of such unburdened individuals is, at least in its own terms, more productive than one based on more traditional households. But we must look closely at why this is so. Both the individual worker and the economic sector as a whole are more productive, at least in part, because they have been allowed to discard the welfare function and to concentrate almost solely on the productive function. We have allowed and even pressured one set of social units to give up the welfare functions, but we have been most reluctant to allow the full responsibility for this necessary activity to be assigned to other units.

The apparent increase of those on welfare is to a significant degree not an increase at all; rather it is a reassignment of the function and responsibility that makes the cost of welfare explicit. Traditional families probably did not know the cost of taking care of Grandmother Jones, much less was the government able to add up such costs for the whole society. But when these costs are shifted to Social Security and Medicare and these are in turn deducted from paychecks, the collectivity suddenly becomes acutely conscious of the aggregate costs of Grandmother Joneses. In short, the major source of our supposedly increased welfare burden is primarily a matter of making explicit costs that under earlier forms of social organization remained largely hidden or disguised.

The point should not, however, be overstated. There have been absolute increases in the need for welfare. In part these have been due to the demand that labor—like all other factors of production in an urban advanced industrial economy—be more nearly uniform and predictable. The pre-World War II family farm (or many a small business) could make use of low-skilled or unreliable labor. The youngest son, George, may have gone on a drunk every weekend and been virtually useless the first part of the week, but by Tuesday or Wednesday the family had him sobered up and got a few days productive work out of him. Moreover even Grandmother Jones made some economic contribution through knitting, mending, and watching the children. In a fully urbanized industrial economy the Grandmother Joneses and the Georges are excluded from both the labor force and the extended household. They cannot meet the minimum levels of skill, predictability, and regularity demanded by bureaucratized work patterns of the labor market, and if they remain attached to a nuclear family they seriously handicap the ability of the other members to participate in such a labor force. Their exclusion from these units does mean that more people are "on welfare" in the most basic sense; they are consuming without actively participating in productive activity.[11] But they are nonparticipants primarily because those controlling the organization of work have found that from the perspective of the work organization (for example, a firm) it is more efficient to exclude them in order to make the labor supply more predictable. The increased percentage of the population on welfare is not primarily due to our altruism toward this subpopulation; it is simply that the rest of us find it more convenient to segregate them from the productive process and the nuclear family.

There are, however, two subsidiary consequences of this move to increase the predictability of the labor force. First, the rate of individual pathologies and the level of care the nonproductive require have probably increased. Since the family sold the farm and moved to town to take factory jobs George does not have anything useful to do even Wednesday through Friday. Moreover the family could not put up with his drunkenness in their small apartment, and so George lives alone—and largely isolated. Now he stays drunk all week—or at least so long as his welfare check lasts. Intermittently he passes out on the street and is taken to the hospital, and this costs the city even more.[12]

But the problem is not simply that the welfare function has been shifted from traditional units or that the number of people on welfare has increased because of the exclusion of the Georges from the productive process. Conservatives are, in a sense, right about there being a decline in "moral fiber" and an increase in "welfare chiselers." This decline in traditional morals is rooted in several structural sources: contradictory role demands (which probably increase people's motivation to deviate), weaker mechanisms of social control, and fewer sources of social solidarity.

With respect to contradictory role demands our productive system requires greater variation and heterogeneity of behavior with respect to actual work, that is, technical specialization. On the other hand greater homogeneity is demanded with respect to the time of participation and level of commitment; that is, one has to show up 8:00 to 5:00, Monday through Friday, sober but not necessarily enthusiastic or devoted. One way of coping with the demands for standardized participation is to take full advantage of one's sick leave—whether or not one is sick—and use one's unemployment benefits to take a vacation between job changes. In small autonomous work units such as family businesses, people knew one another intimately enough to judge accurately the commitment and motivation of others. They could, therefore, decide with reasonable accuracy when some member of the group needed to be excused from productive labor and carried "on welfare" for a while. Moreover, the person on welfare usually had some sense of commitment and solidarity with the productive unit. Perhaps more important he could see very concretely how his long-term interests were linked to the productivity of that unit and how his contribution, or lack of it, affected that productivity. As the organization of both work and welfare has become increasingly complex, bureaucratized, and impersonal, these sources of social control and solidarity have been eroded. Very frequently people are not as committed to their work unit, and they are successful in disguising both their featherbedding on the job and their chiseling when they are on welfare, unemployment, or sick leave. The crucial point is that such behaviors are not a kind of moral measles that one catches from drinking fountains or illicit sex—much less from liberal or leftist literature. They are primarily the consequences of the changes we have made in the way we organize work, that is, the productive function, and in turn the way we have organized the welfare function. For the most part we made these changes because they suited the immediate interest of owners, managers, and those workers who were able to participate in the new modes of economic organization. When you moved from farm to city you did get paid more and you did not have to work as hard. That is, the changes have greatly increased the real income of those participating in the new system, both by increasing the average level of productivity and by relieving them of the burden of participating directly in the welfare function.

On the other hand, the cost of paying for welfare became increasingly onerous. It is one thing to have to put up with George if he is your own brother; it is quite another to have a big piece of your paycheck taken every week for Georges you have never seen, many of whom you rightly suspect could be working if they wanted to. Even harder to take are the moralistic pronouncements of social workers and college professors who make more than you do and who say you should be paying even more in taxes.

Given these various social processes it is hardly surprising the welfare state in America has reached an impasse: more health and welfare services are urgently needed, but there is great reluctance to provide expanded coverage or increased benefits. Moreover resentment is increasing against those who appear to receive benefits without "earning" them.

The point of this overly long but also overly simplified analysis of the welfare function is this: the interorganizational stratification and the largely ineffective strategies of reform we have focused on need to be seen in the context of the broader issue of the appropriate relationship between the productive function and the welfare function. American society must eventually face this issue more explicitly and honestly than has been the case to date.

Chapter Eleven

INTERPRETATIVE REPRISE

In chapter 1, I indicated that, in addition to an analysis of the problems of urban health care, this book would take up three fundamental theoretical questions: (1) how and why does coordination come about (or fail to come about), (2) what are the determinants of social conflict, and (3) what are the sources of social inequality? This chapter summarizes and synthesizes the main findings emerging from my analysis in relation to these questions, though no attempt is made to provide comprehensive answers to such fundamental questions. More specifically the results can be summarized around the following concepts: (1) simplification, (2) neutralization and conflict, and (3) symbiotic inequality. These notions have been central to our discussion, and of course, each parallels one of the three theoretical questions.

SIMPLIFICATION

Much of our analysis has focused on lack of integration, and the resulting neutralization and conflict. These may be common occurrences in the interorganizational order of urban health care systems, but they are not the typical outcome. If they were, social order would be rare in this sector of the society. Inefficient and chaotic as urban health care may seem, the situation does not approach the Hobbesian war of all against all. Moreover, in addition to simply avoiding chaos and maintaining order, this sector of our society manages to achieve a high level of complex, produc-

tive activity. The dominant ideologies and the power structures supporting them may severely restrict use of the simplification mechanisms of
centralized authority and market competition for interorganizational
coordination, but they obviously do not eliminate all integrative mechanisms. What seems to happen is that this sector of the society places a
heavy reliance on particularistic relationships, informal inequality, and
what we have called bastardized mechanisms of integration. By these
means urban health care systems are able to maintain significant—even if
highly inadequate—levels of interorganizational integration and productive activity. Let us now analyze the role of particularism in relation to
our core concepts and propositions. Our question is: given the absence of
the "usual" simplification mechanism, how do particularistic relationships reduce the level of interaction required to maintain a given
level of activity?

Particularism and Simplification

The crux of the matter is indicated in the concept of relationship, that
is, a patterned, relatively stable, ongoing sequence of interaction. When a
relationship is well established, current interaction is maintained in the
context of an already existing set of expectations between the actors.
They know what each other is up to. The most extreme examples are the
highly truncated conversations that take place between close friends and
relatives. Wife: "Did you hear . . . ?" Husband: "Yes, I think we
should . . ." Wife: "I know; I've already called." To an outside listener
such a conversation is devoid of substantive meaning if not completely
nonsensical. But to individuals with an extensive background of shared
experiences the meaning may be completely clear and the conversation
may be the process by which important joint decisions are made. In our
terminology, a previously established relationship greatly reduces the
amount of interaction required for collective decision-making and increases the time available for activity.

This is reflected in at least two ways in our data. First, a tendency to
rely on established relationships was evident even when new arrangements might have "made more sense." This is seen particularly in the
farming-out procedures at Johnson and Bernstein. With respect to back-
up support, Johnson relied on Mercy for neurosurgery, on Mellon for
cardiology, and on University Medical School for pathology. Any one of

these institutions had staff and services in all three areas of more than sufficient quality to provide the services needed by Johnson. Furthermore, Mercy was significantly closer geographically, while Mellon was on the opposite side of town. Why not work out a simpler set of linkages by having all these back-up services performed by one institution? The tendency to leave well enough alone is even more evident for pediatrics. Dr. Mooreman was the chief of pediatrics at both institutions. Nonetheless he used a different set of back-up services for each institution. His comment was, "If there has been one set-up that works well, I haven't changed it, even though it means that they go from here [Johnson] to one place and from Bernstein to the other." Undoubtedly many factors are involved in the tendency of established social relationships to persist. One of the important factors is that well-established particularistic relationships simplify the process of determining the terms of additional joint activity.

Second, there was a clear tendency for interorganizational links to emerge out of interpersonal relationships. It is hard to think of a more commonsense, obvious research finding. However, the interpretation to be given the finding is not self-evident. This cannot be solely explained in terms of individuals' doing favors for one another. Equally important is that these personal ties serve as rudimentary simplification mechanisms reducing the interaction required to establish relationships relevant to interorganizational activity.

But what is the means by which particularistic relationships produce simplification? Earlier we indicated that the two primary bases of simplification seemed to be abstraction and inequality. Particularistic relationships seem to simplify primarily because they involve a special form of abstraction. The mutual expectations developed out of past interactions are, logically speaking, abstract categories shared only by the members of that relationship. For that particular relationship they simplify in the same way that bureaucratic rules do. However, such abstractions tend to be more concrete, ad hoc, and unique than those embodied in universalistic rules. Because of this they are not easily transferable to other relationships. This is, of course, their weakness or limitation as simplification mechanisms.[1] But in other respects this limitation is a strength. Because they are tailor-made for a particular relationship, they communicate more information between the parties involved than do the ready-made, "prepackaged" abstractions of universalistic rules borrowed from the wider culture. We know what our spouse means when he or she says a hotel is "inexpensive." We are much less sure what is meant when the same word is used by a travel agent.

This unreliability of abstract universalistic criteria helps in understanding another aspect of our data. In the discussion of the conflict over particularistic and universalistic criteria I suggested that the greater efficiency of universalism depended on whether one could afford to "play the averages." Universalistic criteria are likely to produce a higher percentage of "correct" decisions when there are a large number of cases. The more standardized the cases are, the more likely this is to be true. However, for any given case, or even a relatively small number of cases, decisions based on the abstract rules may very well produce serious errors. Some cases will not fit the categories. The use of abstractions as a mode of simplification, then, tends to be attractive only when the mistakes can be averaged over a large number of successes. Secondly, universalistic criteria are useful only if it is possible to obtain accurate information relevant to the formal criteria. More specifically the information must enable us to predict future outcomes accurately. For example, does the fact that someone is a high school graduate of the Chicago public school system enable us to make an accurate prediction about his or her skill, honesty, motivation, and the like?

In light of these factors lower class communities' reliance on particularism can be viewed in a somewhat different perspective. In the first place, because of the relatively small number of jobs available, they are not interested in playing the averages. The extreme scarcity characteristic of lower class communities does not afford them the luxury of waiting for a higher level of payoff over the long run. Second, accurate credentials are a characteristic of affluent groups. The formal credentials available in either lower class communities or underdeveloped societies are, on the whole, not very accurate predictors of future behavior. Consequently, even if little or no nepotism were involved—and it certainly is—nonaffluent communities frequently rely on particularistic criteria because in this context abstract rules are not an effective means of simplification.

To illustrate the broader theoretical significance of this perspective, let us introduce a slight tangent into the discussion and use these ideas to analyze briefly an empirical phenomenon not part of our case study of interorganizational relations. In recent years minority groups, women, and the federal government have exerted considerable pressure for equality of opportunity in hiring practices. One aspect of this effort has involved an attack on the so-called "old-boy system": relying on professional colleagues one knows personally as the chief means of determining likely candidates for job openings. This has tended to be standard procedure among the higher status colleges and universities (and probably in the upper echelons of business). Insistence that all faculty openings be publicly advertised, rather than filled through informal interpersonal networks, has often meant academic departments received a large number of applications that had to be processed and evaluated. A department chairman told me that he had received 435 curricula vitae from formally qualified applicants in direct response to an advertisement announcing a single opening for a beginning assistant professor. If only 15 applications are received, which might conceivably be appropriate, approximately 45 people must be contacted for letters of recommendation. Then these letters must be read and evaluated. The evaluation is often difficult, since frequently the reader knows nothing about the writer and has little basis for judging either his competence or his candidness. Hence, decisions must be made on the basis of information of unknown quality, or additional, more "objective" information must be sought. Candidates may be asked to submit samples of their writing, but then these must be read and evaluated. In short, the selection process becomes more complex and burdensome. The point of these observations is not to defend the old-boy system—I am personally opposed to it—but to point out a key source of its perpetuation. It is an important and in some respects a very effective simplification mechanism. I recently heard a colleague remark, "I use the old-boy system because it puts flesh on a curriculum vitae; I know what a letter from a friend means." In our terms the abstractions used in a letter from a friend are "tailor-made" while those of the curriculum vitae are not. I am not suggesting this system of personal selection is free from bias, prejudice, chauvinism, and elitism, but rather that prejudicial factors alone do not account for the persistence of the pattern. If the particularism of the old-boy system is to be replaced by more universalistic procedures, a more effective simplification mechanism must be found or significantly more resources must be devoted to the personnel selection process. We can also predict that the old-boy system will be hardest to root out of highly skilled occupational sectors like academia. In these sectors the work is complex and unstandardized, and it is difficult to measure adequately someone's competence on the basis of the abstract information included on an application form. This is accentuated when the work units to which people are attached are relatively small and each individual is a specialist. Such conditions make academic departments—like ghetto communities—reluctant to "play the averages." The old-boy system, then, is a particularistic simplification mechanism especially well suited to processing complex, unstandardized information relevant to decisions where minimizing the risk of serious error on each and every case is defined as important.

In summary, particularistic relationships provide tailor-made abstractions that reduce the amount of interaction required to integrate expectations about subsequent joint activities. They are a rudimentary mechanism of simplification, but in certain situations they not only are more readily available but also offer distinct advantages over universalistic criteria. However, in the context of modern industrial society a heavy reliance on particularistic relationships is viewed with suspicion. Conventional commonsense explanations attribute nepotism and other forms of particularism to selfishness, immorality, chauvinism, ethnocentrism, ignorance, shortsightedness, ascription, etc.[2] The standard sociological explanation would stress that such behavior is usually rooted in and, in large measure, due to scarcity and poverty. While there are elements of truth in both explanations, this analysis suggests that particularism is relied on, especially as a simplification mechanism, when it is important to reduce uncertainty to a minimum on the specific case at hand—when one cannot afford simply to play the odds over a large number of cases. Scarcity is one source of the need for such certainty but by no means the only one. Therefore we can expect the continuation of such particularism even in highly "rationalized" sectors of society when avoiding uncertainty is considered crucial and we are unable or unwilling to invest extensive resources to create more systematic universalistic knowledge.

Domain Consensus and Particularism

Much of the interorganizational literature has stressed the importance of domain consensus and ideological consensus as prerequisites to coordination and cooperative interorganizational relations.[3] However, Warren has argued that, in fact, domain consensus is rarely an issue, since it is established, not through interaction between particular organizations, but through the conventional understandings acquired from institutional thought structure.[4] Benson claims that, whereas domain and ideological consensus are secondary factors (that is, part of the superstructure) that determine interorganizational relations and coordination, they are ultimately rooted in resource dependencies.[5] Aldrich sees value consensus as the result of interaction, not its prerequisite.[6] In sum, there is a disagreement about the "real" significance of consensus, especially domain consensus for interorganizational relations.

Our data suggest that each factor is a necessary but not sufficient condition for cooperative links. Resource interdependencies are required before there is motivation to interact. For a cooperative relationship to emerge in a voluntaristic context there must be at least an absence of serious disagreement about the domains of the relevant organizations and basic ideology; normally this is provided by the institutionalized thought structure. But in addition to resource dependencies and abstract consensus, relationships are much more likely if previously established particularistic links are available; abstract consensus is a poor substitute for knowing someone you understand and trust.

Warren's data showed only one serious case of domain conflict; this was in the city where the director of the local poverty program called into question the usually accepted institutionalized ideology and seriously threatened conventional values and established interests.[7] In our study serious and sustained conflict arose only when middle- and lower class groups were brought together in what I have called a mandated diffuse linkage. Here, where legal mandates and resource dependencies forced interaction, particularistic relationships became the means to temporarily patch over the lack of institutionalized consensus, but under this strain not even leaders with strong particularistic relationships could last for long. In sum, in the absence of strongly mandated relations both a general institutionalized consensus and particularistic links greatly aid in the establishment and maintenance of interorganizational relations. Under "normal" conditions the second is usually more problematic than the first.

Interorganizational Stratification and Simplification

I have argued that the two elementary means of simplification are abstraction and inequality. Particularistic relationships provide tailor-made abstractions that can be used for simplification when universalistic categories are not available or are considered inapplicable. Similarly the inequality of stratification systems provides simplification mechanisms when more formal authority structures are not available.[8]

The essence of the argument is quite simple. Since formal authority structures and markets operate in a relatively restricted form in the health sector, the informal structures of inequality embodied in the interorganizational stratification system play an important role in the simplification process. First, clear status differences reduce competition and thereby make it easier for organizations to arrive at mutually acceptable expectations about cooperative efforts. For the most part Johnson must decide either to accept Mercy's schedule of fees for scanning procedures or do without these services. Similarly, Johnson's pathologist may be frustrated because University Medical School will not provide more assistance, but he knows that provoking open conflict about the matter would simply lead to the termination of the assistance now provided. He is in a take-it-or-leave-it situation, and this greatly simplifies negotiating and decision-making. Note that the simplification effect of inequality is in addition to, though not independent of, the effect of inequality on resource dependencies. The latter provides motivation for establishing relationships; the former eases the process of negotiating the terms of the relationship. Since we have already examined the matter in considerable detail, we need not belabor the point.

Bastardized Mechanisms

Particularism has, by definition, a crucial limitation as a simplification mechanism: it is restricted to a specific relationship and is difficult to transfer from one actor to another. Consequently, when a large number of different actors must be dealt with, considerable pressure develops to simplify by means other than particularistic relations with each actor. A primary tool for accomplishing this is abstraction. We treat people, decisions, problems, etc. as "cases" that, on the bases of a few characteristics, can be assigned to a particular universalistic category and treated with a standard response.

Universalistic abstractions are relevant to simplification on at least two levels of social organization. The first is what we have referred to as institutional ideology. These ideologies specify the type of simplification mechanisms considered appropriate for a particular type of relationship: market competition for the private sector and coordination for the public sector. The second level is that of actual social relationships, including interorganizational relationships: the specific sets of rules established to govern members of Southwestern Bell Telephone, the rules created by the State Department to govern relationships between its various subunits, or the pattern of relationships that emerges between barbershops in the Atlanta area as a result of the abstractions we use to characterize the commodities they produce, for example, price and convenience.

How accurately abstractions of the first level describe the actual relationships will in large degree be determined by whether or not the distribution of power assumed by the institutional ideologies actually exists. For example, whether the pattern of relationships between barbershops in Atlanta can be predicted from patterns of pricing depends on whether vigorous market competition prevails. Whether the formal rules of the State Department actually describe the patterns of relationships between subunits depends on how much effective power those in the upper levels of the department actually wield.

One of my arguments has been that the distribution of power assumed by the institutional ideologies is much more accurate for some sectors of the society than for others. In what we have called the market system and the government system, the distribution of power approximates that assumed in the institutional ideology.[9] On the other hand, in "the industrial system" the actual distribution of power, especially market power, is much more concentrated than that assumed in the institutional ideology. But when we come to the welfare system, and especially the health sector, the situation is even more complicated; here the institutional ideologies are highly ambiguous about how power is supposed to be distributed. In some senses the whole issue of power is ignored or begged.

At least two results are reflected in our data. First, informal structures of interorganizational stratification play a crucial role in maintaining interorganizational integration. We return to this issue in the following section. Second, the existing simplification structures are often bastardized; that is, the more usual mechanisms of simplification are merged in seemingly peculiar combinations. A highly centralized ambulance dispatch system on the one hand illicitly provides the transportation required for the farming-out system of Johnson, while on the other hand it serves as a latent means of influencing the quasi-market that matches the social status of patients and institutions. In part this bastardization involves the well-known dialectical relationship between formal and informal structures: when the official abstractions do not fit with the concrete realities or when they impinge on some vital interest, latent unofficial patterns are created to cope with these inadequacies.[10] But more is involved than the tension between the official and unofficial patterns. Even on the formal level, structures of authority tend to be ambiguous or involve unusual arrangements. The complicated formal relationships between HEW, Mercy, the city health department, the HCHC staff, and the Southside Health Committee is the most obvious example. The official distribution of power was certainly a bastardized arrangement even if there had been no discrepancy between the formal and informal structures.

In summary, our hypothesis is that the ambiguousness of the institutional ideology regarding the distribution of power plays a significant role in determining the types of simplification mechanisms used. More specifically, the heavy reliance on particularistic relationships and the existence of highly bastardized formal structures are directly related to the vagueness of the institutional ideology. These patterns are not due primarily to the unique factors in the Southside situation or in the history of these institutions.

One final note is required; bastardization does not necessarily have pejorative connotations. I considered using the term "hybrid mechanisms of integration," but "hybrid" has overly positive connotations in the same way that "bastardized" has negative ones. A negative connotation is intended only to the degree that such mechanisms contain incompatible elements that make them ineffective as a means of integration and simplification. To cite one example, the satellite–community participation linkage as it existed in HCHC contained such elements. But I do not mean to imply that the "pure types" of simplification mechanisms are inherently more effective than what I have called bastardized mechanisms.

IDEOLOGIES, NEUTRALIZATION, AND CONFLICT

In the previous section we focused on the existing means of interorganizational integration: on the available but often latent means of simplification that enable the system to work as well as it does. But, as increasing levels of criticism indicate, many in our society perceive our network of health care organizations as poorly integrated. While our ideological formulas call for "greater coordination," attempts to increase interorganizational integration often bog down or even reduce cooperation. The concepts of neutralization and social conflict have been used to describe two types of outcomes that result from aborted attempts to increase integration. Now let us analyze these outcomes in relation to our general theoretical concepts. In this context I will indicate why the ideological formulas intended to encourage integration may increase neutralization and conflict. Finally tentative hypotheses are offered about what determines whether the abortive outcome takes the form of neutralization or conflict.

Complexity and Neutralization

Neutralization typically occurs in situations with a high ratio of interaction to activity; so much interaction is required to produce agreement that nothing gets done. One way this happens is for the complexity of the integration problem to be raised significantly without introducing effective simplification mechanisms. This is often one result of the ideology of coordination. Organizations are encouraged to consult with others that might be affected by their actions. An increasingly large number of actors and issues must be taken into account to actually implement a program. The intent is to reduce duplication and competition. However, since effective simplification mechanisms are not available, the additional resources spent on interaction do not culminate in integrated activity and may be more costly than the duplication and competition. Our study has no data bearing directly on this issue. It seems reasonably clear, however, that ideological formulas stressing the need for coordination (and complaining about duplication and waste) tend to ignore the cost of producing effective integration, as well as the waste stemming from neutralization. More accurately these costly negative outcomes are given various ad hoc explanations and are not seen as, in part, the result of our oversimplified and contradictory ideological formulas.

At least three cases of neutralization were described. One was the effort to secure additional x-ray equipment for the Heightsville Community Health Center. No one opposed this, as a matter of principle, but so many actors and issues had to be fitted together that the negotiation and decision-making process could not be finalized. The attempt to avoid duplication and waste by increased cooperation and coordination meant decisive action became impossible, and a stalemate over relatively trivial issues resulted. The second case involved the attempt to institute an ambulance service at Mercy. By the time that the interests and problems of Johnson, the city ambulance service, and the various departments of Mercy were dealt with, more than three years had elapsed and the prospects for a new ambulance service were still doubtful. To some extent a third bit of our data can be analyzed from this perspective. The plan for Johnson and Bernstein to merge and build a new health park has in some respects come to a halt because of neutralization. Admittedly the major obstacle is simply a lack of resources. The poor chances of acquiring needed resources are, however, related to the inability of the two hospitals to reach a consensus and pursue the matter jointly. This stems from conflicts of interest, for example, the insecurity and rivalry of the two administrators. But the sheer complexity of the issue is also a factor. Particularly troublesome is that Bernstein is a city institution, while Johnson is a voluntary hospital. This makes especially difficult the creation of an authority structure with the power and legitimacy needed to resolve the issues. The exhortation is once again more coordination, but without the necessary mechanisms of simplification. As a result the plans have not been abandoned, but they have been indefinitely postponed.

Ideological assumptions contribute to neutralization in yet another way. The standard strategy of reform is to create new programs to meet the needs of the disadvantaged. HCHC is, of course, the example on which we have concentrated. But Mac Brown alone was involved in half a dozen new neighborhood organizations. Dr. Warren, the founder of HCHC, was successful in creating four or five other new programs. In short, reform efforts tend to increase the number of organizational actors in a given area. In our theoretical terms this means that complexity increases and in turn integration becomes even more difficult. But the effect of this reform strategy does not stop here. Many of these new programs are "demonstration projects" or "experimental." Consequently they seldom have long-term legitimacy and funding. More often than not they operate for a few years, are discontinued, and eventually are in part replaced by some new program. Sarah Jones, the head of the social work department at Johnson, called them "meteors" or "TNT organizations." Personnel and organizations come and go relatively quickly. This high turnover means that particularistic relationships, the most rudimentary mechanism for integration, are necessarily weakened and reduced —further contributing to neutralization and lack of integration.

Social Conflict

Some of the sources of interorganizational conflict can also be explained by this same frame of reference. Neutralization involves withdrawing from nonproductive interaction, but, in contrast, conflict involves the intensification of interaction by the use of negative sanctions. That is, one actor punishes another actor to persuade him to behave in a more acceptable manner. The inability to obtain integration is seen as the failure of the other actor to conform to legitimate expectations.[11] But at least in the case of HCHC the cause of this inability to develop mutually acceptable expectations often emanated from the same source as neutralization. Ideological formulas encourage the creation of complex sets of relationships without providing adequate mechanisms for simplification and the resolution of disputes. In the case of HCHC there were, in addition to the ideology of coordination, two additional ideological formulas contributing to a high level of complexity. Both the stress on community participation and the assumed superiority of nongovernmental institutions added to the complexity of the interorganizational network. Clearly a clinic operated directly by the city's health department without a community board would have greatly reduced the complexity of the integration problem. I am not suggesting this would have been the appropriate policy to follow; rather I am pointing to the sociological consequences of the policy pursued and to how policy was rooted in the institutionalized ideological formulas.

To add to the difficulties, the simplification mechanisms formally available were themselves a source of conflict. That is, the distribution of authority was highly ambiguous; there was disagreement over who had the right to "simplify" the decision-making. Mercy claimed final authority and saw the role of the Southside Committee as advisory. The committee, of course, rejected this interpretation and increasingly demanded broader powers for itself. In short, the right to "simplify" by exercising formal authority became an issue itself and added to, rather than reduced, the complexity of the integration problem. Moreover, the ambiguities over the appropriate distribution of authority reflected, to a considerable degree, the ambiguities and contradictions embodied in the ideological formulas of community participation.

Neutralization or Conflict

Even if it is granted that the ideological formulas tend to increase complexity and that complexity increases the likelihood of incompatible and conflicting expectations, what determines whether the outcome is neutralization or overt social conflict? One factor is obviously important: the degree of conflict on the level of more abstract norms and values. Our focus has been on the integration of activity, and as repeatedly stated, there is no assumption that the integration of activity requires actors to share similar sentiments, basic norms, or generalized values. On the other hand, social systems that do have a consensus about basic values usually have an easier time integrating activities. In the case of HCHC the ideology of community participation was particularly significant in bringing contradictory values into conflict. The orientations of the various bureaucratic officials and of the representatives of the local community differ in many respects, but a particularly critical problem was the different emphases placed on particularism and universalism. This was especially evident with regard to the criteria and procedures for hiring nonprofessional staff. A lack of integration at the level of basic orientations increases the probability of overt conflict.

A second factor also seemed important in the Southside situation. The parties in the HCHC network could not simply withdraw from the relationship. They were linked together in what I have called a mandated diffuse relationship. That is, the relationship was both involuntary and broad in scope. Mercy and the Southside Committee had to deal with each other about a wide array of important issues. Neither side was free to seek a "better deal" elsewhere if dissatisfied with the terms of the relationship. The only alternatives, in the short run, were capitulation or conflict—to tolerate the existing situation or to force the other side to change the nature of the relationship. Much of the conflict described involves the committee's using negative sanctions against Mercy as a means of motivating the hospital to grant the committee actual authority. Usually these sanctions took the form of creating public disturbances embarrassing to Mercy. The significance of the mandated diffuse linkage for social conflict is by no means limited to interorganizational relationships between health organizations. For example, the differences in the intensity of conflict likely to develop within a marriage as contrasted to a casual dating relationship can be understood in these terms. Marriage relationships are very diffuse and not easily terminated. Consequently there is both a greater probability that serious disagreement will arise and that the parties will "fight out" the issue rather than simply terminate the relationship. In a dating relationship serious disagreement is less likely, and if it does occur the probable result will be the termination of the relationship rather than prolonged, bitter conflict.

Even more common than conflict between Mercy and the committee was conflict revolving around the boundary personnel responsible for mediating the hospital–committee linkage. Interorganizational conflict was to some extent muted by being transformed into role conflict. But as a result positions on the boundary became lightning rods, and no one was secure in such a position for long.

Summary

The ideologies that stressed coordination, community participation, and the efficacy of nongovernmental organizations encouraged the creation of highly complex interorganizational relationships. But these same ideologies made the creation of adequate simplification and dispute settlement mechanisms difficult. This was due in part to the contradictions built into the ideological formulas. For example, the ideology of coordination stresses the legitimacy of both cooperation and organizational autonomy. The ideology of community participation stresses the right of local communities to "participate" in decision-making but leaves vague the actual distribution of authority. The ideology stressing the greater efficiency of nongovernmental organizations ignores how this supposed efficacy is rooted in the nongovernmental agencies' ability to limit the demands placed on them. A common result of these ideological and structural contradictions is social conflict and what I have called neutralization. Two factors seem important in determining which of these unintended outcomes is more likely. A lack of integration at the level of general norms and values (for example, the differential emphases on particularism and universalism) increases the chances that difficulties in integrating activities will lead to overt conflict. Secondly, conflict is likely the more explicitly monopolistic and exclusive the linkage, that is, in mandated diffuse links. Where these factors are less prevalent, neutralization seems to be the more likely outcome.

Deviance, Conformity, and Inefficiency

Why does the health-care delivery system seem to be so uncoordinated and inefficient? Conventional wisdom tends to place the blame on the incompetence of individuals and the flaws of the public sector. The skill and commitment of the staff serving in poor-quality institutions are seen as the source of the difficulty. Perhaps this in turn is explained in terms of the absence of a profit motive or the "inevitable" inefficiencies of government or quasi-government bureaucracies. Some conflict analyses attribute the problems to the efforts of specific subgroups within the health-care system to self-consciously defend and advance their self-interest. Consequently the failure of various reform efforts is explained by cooptation or diversion; professionals of various sorts make sure that reform efforts are directed into channels that are relatively harmless to vested interests. In both of these explanations failure is seen as a form of deviance; inefficiency and inequality result because various actors fail to live up to the societal norms. In the first case the direct providers of services are not sufficiently committed or appropriately rewarded. In the second case various subgroups of elites of the health care system are in some senses cynical; they allow others to play at reform, but they have no intention of allowing changes detrimental to their interest. They do not believe in or seriously intend to follow the goals and norms they publicly espouse. I have suggested a third possibility: that both elites and nonelites often do attempt to conform to the institutionalized norms, that they often do seek to increase interorganizational communication and coordination, but that this very conformity results in neutralization, conflict, and inefficiency. To a significant degree the problem is not deviance but conformity. This interpretation is not offered as a complete substitute for the other perspectives; obviously the first two explanations contain significant elements of truth. However, the nature of the health care system will be inadequately understood if we see its problems primarily as deviance rather than as the result of institutionalized structures.

SYMBIOTIC INEQUALITY

Resource Dependency Perspective

Let us begin our discussion by briefly summarizing the way that the relationship between Mercy Hospital and Johnson Hospital might be analyzed from Pfeffer and Salancik's resource dependency perspective.[12] Because Mercy and Johnson are in the same industry, they are supposedly in competition with each other. Consequently how concentrated that industry is—whether there are only a few or many producers—will determine the nature of their interorganizational relationships. Very low concentration would result in relatively little direct interdependence, and for all practical purposes any given producer could be safely ignored by the others, at least in the short run. If the industry were highly concentrated they might have high interdependence but would more than likely handle this by informal, tacit agreement not to threaten each other's welfare seriously. If there was an intermediate level of concentration they would probably manage their interdependence through some more formal agency such as a coordinating council. Or possibly the dominant institutions might try to reduce uncertainty by absorbing the weaker institutions. For all practical purposes these outcomes have not occurred. Despite the fact that Mercy and Johnson are in the same industry, even when the industrial category is very narrowly defined, they are not primarily in competition with each other, because of interorganizational inequality, especially differences in prestige. They serve a different clientele and in many respects provide different services. One concentrates on research, teaching, treatment of esoteric cases, and services to the upper and middle class; the other primarily provides minimum levels of care to the lower class. Moreover, it is essential for the low-status hospital to perform its function or the high-status hospital would be over-whelmed with demands from the lower class; it could not give high-quality care or focus its attention on research, teaching, and esoteric cases.

In terms of the resource dependency perspective this means that the two institutions might be more accurately considered to be in symbiotic rather than competitive interdependence. Under this condition the re-source dependency perspective would predict that if there was high in-terdependence and high uncertainty, the dominant institution would move toward vertical integration—assuming no prohibition against it. That is, it would attempt to merge with the other organization or by growth gain direct control over the problematic functions. But this is not what happens either. The two institutions retain separate identities. The dominant institution takes various informal measures, on the one hand, to maintain its prestige and dominance and, on the other hand, to give its weaker neighbor assistance and protection and thereby ensure its con-tinued separate existence. This outcome results because in the existing interorganizational and societal stratification system Johnson's functions are poorly supported and rewarded, while Mercy's functions receive high support and rewards.

This situation has been referred to as symbiotic inequality. But before this concept can be more fully specified we must turn our attention briefly to some issues in stratification theory.

Three Bases of Distribution

Within stratification theory there are supposedly two main perspec-tives. The conflict perspective sees inequalities of power and privilege fundamentally rooted in exploitation. Marx and, to some degree, Pareto, and their intellectual descendants are usually associated with this per-spective. The functionalist view maintains that inequalities of power and privilege are primarily based on differential conformity to collective, consensual norms. Such names as Emile Durkheim, Talcott Parsons, Kingsley Davis, and Wilbur Moore are usually linked with this position.

I suggest that part of the processes described under the concept sym-biotic inequality represent a third perspective, which if not of equal im-portance, is nonetheless crucial to understanding some aspects of social inequality. This outlook stresses the significance of the resources needed for survival. Of course, this is not a new idea; Lenski makes need one of his two principles of distribution underlying stratification.[13]

Before I elaborate the significance of need, Lenski's second principle of distribution—power—requires discussion. More specifically it must be decomposed and related to the conflict and functionalist perspectives. In certain respects both the functionalists and the conflict theorists agree that stratification is rooted in inequalities of power—when power is broadly conceived. The crucial argument is over the source of differential power. For functionalists the general source of that power is differential conformity to norms and particularly differential performance. Those who make the greatest contribution to the consensual definition of the common good are most powerful because they are most valuable to the collectivity. Consequently they receive the highest levels of reward, in part because they are admired and appreciated, and in part because the dependence of others on their contributions gives them the power to demand higher rewards. Stated another way, for the functionalist the predominant type of power is legitimate power acquired through conformity to norms. Depending on the theorist involved this argument is used to explain inequality between individuals or social positions or both.

For the conflict theorist power is only weakly related to one's conformity to consensual norms and contribution to the common good. Stated another way the predominant type of power is illicit if not illegitimate in the sense that it is based on deception, manipulation, inherited advantage, and coercion. Significant differences in power develop primarily by cheating, bending or rigging the rules, luck, or the ability to coerce others. In short, as Lenski claims—though not in exactly the manner presented here—his theory combines both the functionalist and the conflict perspective.

To some degree, in all societies power (and its accompanying status and privilege) is acquired by both legitimate and illegitimate means. Even in the most tyrannical and corrupt regimes power cannot be maintained if norms are totally ignored. On the other hand utopian societies, where all behavior is governed by legitimate norms, do not exist. In most social systems some of the power is acquired by legitimate social processes, while some is acquired by nonlegitimate means. The extent to which one source of power is predominant within a given social system or for a specific actor will, of course, vary tremendously.

But there is a third theme in stratification theory that emphasizes the significance of the minimum needs for survival as a principle governing the distribution of resources. It is explicit in Lenski's theory. The key notion is that even those actors who have no power—either legitimate or illegitimate—should receive enough of the collective resources to ensure their survival. To some degree this need principle is based on a special kind of power. The services of the actors involved are valuable enough so that the privileged do want them to continue in existence. This is what I have referred to as symbiotic inequality. But generally the power that an actor can secure by threatening suicide, or pointing out that death will occur if he does not receive more resources, is quite limited. The need principle is also to some degree based on conformity to norms. At the very least the actor must have the characteristics that conform to the membership requirements of at least some vague social system such as humankind. To receive resources because of need, actors must usually conform to norms demanding expressions of gratitude and subservience. Despite the elements of the other two principles, I believe it is useful to treat this as a third basic process of distribution.

This foray into general stratification theory may seem as out of place as it is truncated. I introduce it because there are examples of all three types of processes in the patterns of interorganizational stratification we have examined. Let us begin with the functional model. Mercy Hospital's performance (conformity) is clearly perceived to be greater than Johnson's or Bernstein's, and this perception results in higher status. As conceptualized here power is the sum total of all forms of influence available to an actor. Status, resources, and force are on a lower level of abstraction. Consequently status is an important source of power because it usually makes an actor attractive to other actors—they want to "associate" with the high-status actor. In this case patients and staff are more attracted to high-status than to low-status hospitals, other factors being equal. This enables Mercy to be selective in the sense that they admit relatively large numbers of patients able to pay the full cost of their care. This leads to higher rewards (income from patients), which is one of the major sources of Mercy's generally higher resource base (wealth). These higher resources in turn are a major source of Mercy's higher levels of performance. By using an arrow (→) to mean "leads to" or "contributes to," the argument can be summarized in the following manner: performance → status → attractiveness → ability to select clients → rewards → resources → performance. There are, of course, sources of higher performance other than resource base, but the nature of our data have not allowed us to deal with these. (Management skills, for example, undoubtedly play some role.) My point is not that this is a completely adequate explanation of inequality even if the functional perspective is accepted. Rather I want to show that functional processes explain at least some of the interorganizational inequality we have observed.

In contrast, other aspects of inequality are better understood with the conflict perspective. The generalized power Mercy secures through high status and high resources was frequently used to bias the organization of the interorganizational network. That is, "routine" processes are structured—whether consciously or unconsciously—so as to contribute to the maintenance and expansion of Mercy's privileges. In this case the illegitimate power to bias the system often operated through its effects on client selectivity. For example, the organization of the ambulance service contributed to channeling desirable patients to Mercy. A second example was Mercy's power to maintain outpatient departments that were little better with respect to their "human quality"—convenience and consideration for the patients—than low status hospitals. This enabled Mercy to lower the attractiveness of their institution to undesirable patients, and this tactic in turn affected selectivity. In short, to some extent the distribution of resources within the interorganizational network is rooted in the ability of some actors to use illegitimate power to "rig" things in their favor.

For the most part our analysis stressed the third type of process—distribution according to need. I have focused on this, not because it is the primary process, but because it was initially the most puzzling. Two chains of influence are at work here. The ability of high-status institutions to select their patients leads to functional differentiation—some institutions are forced to "specialize" in the treatment of undesirable patients. But this differentiation produces a type of dependence. Low-status institutions perform a necessary activity that to some degree the high-status institutions would have to assume if the low-status ones did not exist. The second chain of influence is due to the unequal distribution of resources resulting from the conflict and functional processes described above. The very existence of the low-status institutions is threatened because of their inability to gain even minimal success in either the legitimate or illegitimate forms of competition for power. The threatened extinction of needed lower status actors results in redistribution processes and self-imposed limitations on the exercise of power. Examples include the cooperation of the higher status institutions with Johnson's farming-out system and Mercy's concern not to take away Johnson's ambulance service. This redistribution process to some extent modifies the allocation of resources resulting from the functional and conflict processes, which in turn marginally modifies the distribution of power. Need is treated as a separate major process because the redistribution cannot be adequately explained in the usual terms of either the functional or conflict model—unless the concepts of conformity and coercion are defined so broadly as to become virtually meaningless or tautological. I do not mean to claim that need is equally important in all systems of stratificaiton, much less that the specific propositions relevant to this interorganizational network are universally valid. I am suggesting that stratification theory may well benefit from further attempts to analyze systems of inequality in terms of these three bases of distribution. But lest I seem to be implying that need is the crucial element of symbiotic inequality let us turn to its more coercive aspects.

The Forced Division of Labor

Two primary criticisms are leveled against functional explanations of inequality. The simplest argument is that rewards are gained primarily by outright coercion and cheating. Those with power use extortion to get what they want, or they use their power to hide their illicit acquisition of privileges. A second criticism is that those with power gain their privileges by fooling other people into thinking that the activities they perform are especially important and deserve high rewards. The critics argue there is very little if any objective basis for believing one set of human activities is innately more valuable than any other. Those with power are able to shape the definition of what is important and valuable. However, recent work by Treiman finds a great deal of uniformity across cultures in the prestige attributed to different types of activities. This makes it, of course, more difficult to simply dismiss the notion of objective functional importance.[14] But serious questions about the functional theory of inequality are in order without resorting to either the

cynicism of the first critique or the extreme cultural relativity implied by
the second. A third criticism of functional theory avoids the difficulties
of cynicism and relativism and is compatible with the data presented.
Durkheim's phrase "the forced division of labor" (if not his precise meaning) describes the process rather well. Those with power gain privileges
primarily by reserving for themselves the functions that, in any given
historical period, are objectively more important for maintaining and improving the collective welfare. This is not to say the powerful never use
blatant coercion to gain illegitimate privilege or never exaggerate the importance of what they do. But at least in some situations the primary
root to privilege is by identifying and monopolizing the jobs likely to be
highly valued and casting off on others those which are not valued. This
seems to be the strategy used by the dominant health care institutions in
urban America. According to Wallerstein, it was also the primary strategy of the nations that successfully began the modernization process in
the sixteenth century.[15] It is hardly a new idea to suggest monopoli-
zation of valued activities is a means to power and privilege. Discussions
of rising and falling elites at least from Pareto on have relied heavily on
these notions. In part it is why so much attention has been paid to mobility and equality of opportunity. Nonetheless discussions of inequality
in America typically see the distribution of privilege primarily as resulting from the division of labor. We would, however, probably get further
in our understanding if we at least in some situations reversed this
sequence and attempted to see the division of labor as deriving from the
structure of power and privilege.

Latent Power and Stability

Why has the existing structure of relationships with its inequality and
inefficiencies tended to persist? Why, if urban health care systems have
been in "crisis" for twenty years or more, has the pattern of relations
remained largely unchanged? If competition, conflict, and neutralization
are common occurrences, why do we continue to rely on particularistic
relationships and informal structures of stratification as primary mechanisms of integration? Finally, why does the ideology of coordination continue to provide legitimacy for the existing structures when there has
been relatively little improvement in reducing fragmentation of health
care delivery despite considerable reform efforts?

We have considered the existing interorganizational inequality as both a simplification mechanism and as a particular mode of dominance (that is, symbiotic inequality). But what is the relationship between these two aspects of inequality? In large measure the first makes the second feasible. To state the matter another way, if the more explicit simplification mechanism of a formal authority structure were substituted for the informal inequality of interorganizational stratification, the latent structures of symbiotic inequality would be more difficult to justify and maintain. In liberal democracies it is difficult to formalize power differences into explicit authority structures without doing the same for the structures of privilege. If authority is explicitly assigned, the scope of that authority and the nature of the concomitant privileges are made relatively explicit. Weber's classic ideal-type model of bureaucracy involves not only a specified hierarchy but also "strictly delimited" authority and the clear separation of personal and official property.[16] To illustrate the proposition in terms of the system we have been studying, let us perform a "mental experiment." Suppose that Johnson hospital became an official branch of Mercy subject to its formal authority. Could Mercy allow the existing differences in quality and scope of service to continue and still maintain its own legitimacy and prestige? The answer is almost certainly no. Such behavior would be viewed as inexcusable and intolerable. The relationship with HCHC was, therefore, much more problematic than the relationship with Johnson. Yet certainly Johnson and its 100,000 outpatients were much more crucial to Mercy's welfare than HCHC. Informal stratification can offer many advantages for the privileged—especially in societies that have strong egalitarian ideologies.

Now we are able to deal more directly with why the contradiction between the ideology emphasizing coordination and the actual structural realities has persisted for so long. Given the current funding arrangements it is clearly to the advantage of high-status institutions not to create a more integrated or formalized system. The more formally health care institutions are tied together, the greater would be the pressure to equalize the distribution of resources within the interorganizational system. On the other hand, high-status institutions cannot publicly advocate duplication and inefficiency. They are, in fact, genuinely opposed to inefficiency—where the elimination of such waste does not also mean the elimination of their own privilege and prestige. Nor would the return to market competition work to their advantage. Dominant groups may recommend to others the invigorating thrill of unrestrained competition, but they are usually willing to forgo these pleasures themselves. The strong cultural suspicion of those who unabashedly make a profit from serving the sick and incapacited is an additional reason for not defining market competition as the appropriate mode of interorganizational relationships. In this context a strong verbal commitment to "increased coordination" and a continuing reliance on particularistic relationships and the informal influence of stratification structures are a most understandable response.

In short, the contradiction between the ideology and actual patterns of interorganizational integration makes possible the structures of interorganizational stratification that characterize many urban health systems. These structures of stratification, along with particularistic links, are a convenient means of balancing the need for minimum levels of interorganizational integration and the understandable desire of the high-status institutions to maintain their prestige, privilege, and an enclave of high-quality care and research.

Now in concluding our discussion of symbiotic inequality it is possible to offer a more systematic specification of the concept. The notion refers to the three elements discussed in the last three subsections. Under conditions of symbiotic inequality structures of power and privilege are largely latent and informal. To a considerable extent there is a "forced division of labor." Finally, dominant actors not only take actions to maintain their own power and privilege, but they also go to considerable pains to ensure that the minimal needs of the weak and underprivileged are met. From the point of view of dominant actors the combination of these three attributes seems to be a highly effective mechanism of social stratification.

THE FUTURE

Let us carry the analysis one step further and speculate about why this system of interorganizational stratification is accepted by the broader political structures. The willingness of the general public to tolerate this interorganizational stratification is at least in part rooted in the fact that up to now the situation has been tolerable, if not ideal, for the upper and middle classes. The reform of health care has not been a high priority for these classes. Moreover, they seem to be aware that the resources required to create a more equitable system will be substantial. Equally important, given our tax structure, the cost would be extracted primarily from the middle class. Until the "crisis" in health care seriously affects the privileged groups in our society, major structural changes seem unlikely; reform will not result because of exposés of the horrors of health care for the poor. Rather it will probably come about—if it comes at all—because of skyrocketing costs and the reduction of services for the middle class resulting from efforts to hold down costs. In metropolitan areas these increased costs and reduced services will result, in part, from the collapse of lower status hospitals. Even with help from high-status hospitals in the form of symbiotic inequality, it seems likely that many of the lower status institutions will be unable to survive the contradictory pressures to which they are subject—for example, demands by citizens and politicians for both an end to the recurring horror stories and scandals, and an end to continual budget increases.

To the degree that lower status health care institutions do go out of business, or reduce the scope of their services, higher status institutions will have to serve a higher proportion of poor people. Unless there is a substantial change in the way health care is funded and organized, several outcomes are probable. First, middle- and upper-class patients will be charged even higher fees to cover the cost of those who cannot pay. This will, of course, result in even more complaints about health costs being out of control. Second, there is likely to be additional internal stratification in the formerly high-status metropolitan hospitals—though institutions will probably go to considerable lengths to disguise this. Third, where several high-status institutions are in the same general area they may merge their emergency and outpatient services. The purpose of this will be described in terms of "coordination" and "economies of scale," but this will also limit the access of low-income patients and reduce the possibility of comparing, and therefore judging, the performance of institutions in comparable settings. Finally, contradictory pressures to serve the poor and reduce cost are likely to make the traditional high-status metropolitan hospital a very difficult institution to maintain and operate. If this results in a significant reduction in services to the middle class, it may well contribute to a social and political dynamic that affects far more than health care.

NOTES

PREFACE

1. Murray Milner, Jr., *The Illusion of Equality* (San Francisco: Jossey-Bass, 1972).
2. Eliot Freidson, *Professional Dominance: The Social Structure of Medical Care* (New York: Atherton, 1970). See also his *Profession of Medicine* (New York: Dodd, Mead, 1970).

1. THE GROUNDWORK

1. Material in the second quotation is made available through the courtesy of Mr. Barry Siegel.
2. David Mechanic, "A Conceptual Approach," in Charles E. Lewis, Roshi Fein, and David Mechanic, *A Right to Health: The Problems of Access to Primary Medical Care* (New York: Wiley, 1976), p. 8.
3. Charles E. Lewis, "Past History," in Charles E. Lewis et al., *ibid.*, pp. 243–44.
4. Robert R. Alford, *Health Care Politics: Ideological and Interest Group Barriers to Reform* (Chicago: University of Chicago Press, 1975), pp. 262–66.
5. Among sociologists Eliot Freidson's position approximates this perspective. See Freidson, *Professional Dominance: The Social Structure of Medical Care* (New York: Atherton, 1970).
6. Alford, *Health Care Politics*, pp. 265–66. Another book which uses a class perspective is Elliott A. Krause's *Power and Illness* (New York: Elsevier, 1977). Unfortunately Krause's book came to my attention after the manuscript for this book was completed. There are a number of parallels in our analyses. Krause, however, focuses more on aspects of the health care system, while this book is more closely tied to interorganizational analysis and, to some degree, gives greater attention to more abstract theoretical issues. Krause's approach is explicitly Marxist while mine is not—though it is heavily influenced by this perspective. It is in some respects encouraging that two social scientists using different theoretical approaches and working independently arrive at roughly similar conclusions about the structure and dynamics of the existing health care system.
7. *Ibid.*, p. 266.

8. David Mechanic, *The Growth of Bureaucratic Medicine* (New York: Wiley, 1976), pp. 6off.

9. Actually Mechanic's remarks are directed to a slightly earlier version of Alford's analysis: Robert R. Alford, "The Political Economy of Health Care: Dynamics Without Change," *Politics and Society* (1972), 2:124–64. The argument of the two versions is, however, fundamentally the same.

10. Mechanic, *Growth of Bureaucratic Medicine*, pp. 61–62.

11. Gerhard E. Lenski, *Power and Privilege* (New York: McGraw-Hill, 1966).

12. See, for example, Alvin Gouldner, "Reciprocity and Autonomy in Functional Theory," in Llewellyn Gross, ed., *Symposium on Sociological Theory*, (Evanston, Ill.: Row and Peterson, 1959); Sol Levine and Paul E. White, "Exchange as a Conceptual Framework for the Study of Interorganizational Relationships," *Administrative Science Quarterly* (March 1961), 5:583–601; Michael Aiken and Jerald Hage, "Organizational Interdependence and Intraorganizational Structure," in Merlin B. Brinkerhoff and Philip R. Kunz, eds., *Complex Organizations and Their Environments* (Dubuque, Iowa: Wm. C. Brown, 1972), pp. 367–94. In dealing with individuals, the assumption of a clear preference for autonomy over interdependence is admittedly a problematic oversimplification, though probably more accurate than the opposite assumption. When, however, we are dealing with collectivities, such as organizations, the assumption is a much more tolerable one. While individuals may have some innate need for interdependence and a significant capacity to identify with the needs of others, these characteristics seem to be considerably weaker at the collective level. Probably the best discussion of this difference in individual and collective attributes is still Reinhold Niebuhr's *Moral Man and Immoral Society* (New York: Scribner's, 1932). Collectivities do, of course, sometimes choose to increase their interdependence, but this seldom happens when "all other things are equal."

13. J. Kenneth Benson, "The Interorganizational Network as a Political Economy," *Administrative Science Quarterly* (June 1975), 20:229–49; Howard Aldrich, "Resource Dependence and Interorganizational Relations," *Administration and Society* (1976), 4:419–53; Jeffrey Pfeffer and Gerald R. Salancik, *The External Control of Organizations* (New York: Harper & Row, 1978).

14. J. Kenneth Benson, "The Interorganizational Network," pp. 229–49.

15. Sol Levine and Paul E. White, "Exchange as a Conceptual Framework for the Study of Interorganizational Relationships," *Administrative Science Quarterly* (March 1961), 5:583–601; Eugene Litwak and L. F. Hylton, "Interorganizational Analysis: A Hypothesis on Coordinating Agencies," *Administrative Science Quarterly* (March 1962), 6:395–420; Michael Aiken and Jerald Hage, "Organizational Interdependence and Intraorganizational Structure," *American Sociological Review* (December 1962), 33:912–30; Herman Turk, "Interorganizational Networks in Urban Society," *American Sociological Review* (February 1970), 35:1–19; Roland Warren, "The Interorganizational Field as a Focus for Investigation," *Administrative Science Quarterly* (December 1967), 12:396–419.

16. Alvin Gouldner, *Patterns of Industrial Bureaucracy* (Glencoe, Ill.: Free Press, 1954); Peter Blau, *The Dynamics of Bureaucracy*, rev. ed. (Chicago: University of Chicago Press, 1963); Philip Selznick, *TVA and the Grassroots* (New York: Harper Torch Books, [1949], 1966). There is a renewed interest in qualitative methodologies for the study of organizations. After this book was in press, *Administrative Science Quarterly* (December 1979), 24(4) devoted an entire issue to this subject.

17. Roland Warren et al., *The Structure of Urban Reform: Community Decision Organizations in Stability and Change* (Lexington, Massachusetts: Lexington Books, 1974).

18. For the classic statement of this position, see Karl Mannheim, *Ideology and Utopia* (New York: Harcourt Brace, 1936). Two other important works concerning this tradition are Robert K. Merton, *Social Theory and Social Structure* (Glencoe, Ill.: Free Press, 1957), chaps. 12–13, and Peter Berger and Thomas Luckmann, *The Social Construction of Reality* (Garden City, N.Y.: Doubleday, 1966).

19. Supposedly the selection of the level of analysis mediates the relationship between the observer's social position and his knowledge. That is, one's social position influences which level of social organization one chooses to study, and this selection in turn influences what one "knows" about the social structure.

20. A parallel methodological issue has arisen in the study of "modernization." Initial attempts to understand the development of modern states and economic systems emphasized the comparative method in which each nation-state was treated as a separate case. When data about enough cases were available, this approach lent itself to quantitative statistical analysis. Some more recent analyses—especially the work of Immanuel Wallerstein (*The Modern World-System: Capitalist Agriculture and the Origins of the European World Economy in the Sixteenth Century* [New York: Academic Press, 1974])—have emphasized that "modernization" involves the creation of an interrelated world-system. Each different nation-state is not an independent case but a specialized and sometimes unique part of a broader system. Consequently, for at least some purposes there is only one case—the world-system—that must be analyzed interpretatively rather than by quantitative comparisons. My position is that both approaches have some validity, depending on the issue under analysis, and are supplementary rather than mutually exclusive alternatives. I take the same view with respect to the interorganizational analysis of health care organizations. Quantitative analyses treating separate institutions, pairs of institutions, or organizational sets as single cases have been valuable. But they have an inherent limitation. Consequently analyses treating individual cases as part of a complex larger system are also needed, and these are necessarily more dependent on qualitative data and analyses. Of course this mode of analysis also has its inherent limitations.

21. See Randall Collins, *Conflict Sociology* (New York: Academic Press, 1975), chap. 1, for a discussion of creating a scientific sociology.

3. A CENTRALIZED AUTHORITY STRUCTURE

1. For the seminal definition of particularism see Talcott Parsons and Edward Shils, eds., *Toward a General Theory of Action* (Cambridge: Harvard University Press, 1951), pp. 81–83. For interaction or a social relationship to be particularistic does not mean that it is necessarily personal, affective, or ascribed. Rather, the core idea is that one actor treats the other as having a unique identity. For example, even an impersonalistic relationship between General Motors and Ford Motors is relatively particularistic, but the relation between GM and its various local dealers is much less particularistic.

There are parallels between my discussion of particularistic interaction and Strauss's discussion of a negotiated order (Anselm Strauss et al., "The Hospital as a Negotiated Order," in Eliot Freidson, ed., *The Hospital in Modern Society* [New York: Free Press, 1963]). Strauss's discussion, however, is largely confined to interpersonal relations within a psychiatric hospital. I have chosen to use the concept of particularistic interaction, rather than Strauss's terminology, in order to clearly differentiate the concept and more systematically relate it to the other mechanisms of simplification to be discussed shortly.

2. Since the concept of integration is controversial and has varied meanings in social theory, some further specification is required. By integration of activity, I mean the avoidance of mutually impossible modes of action, so that the activities of one actor do not interfere with the activities of other actors. When we both keep to the right, my driving down the street in one direction does not interfere with your driving down the same street in the other direction. When I talk about the integration of joint activity, I mean that not only do we avoid actions that interfere with each other, but we also direct our actions so that they contribute to some "common goal." By "common goal" I do not necessarily mean that the actors endorse or share the goal, nor do I assume that the integration of joint activity is based on value consensus. An illustration should clarify this matter. Imagine that two people who hate each other are to be executed. One may be forced at gunpoint to build a scaffold while the other is forced to dig two graves. In this situation their joint activities are integrated in our sense of the word: their actions do not interfere with one another and they contribute to some common goal—though hardly one they share. The only value consensus necessary either between themselves or their captors is that they had rather postpone their death for a little while by carrying out these tasks than be shot dead on the spot. (According to Ollman, Marx used the term "cooperation" in this same sense. See Bertell Ollman, *Alienation* [Cambridge: Cambridge University Press, 1971].)

3. For a useful discussion of the various types of interorganizational coordinating arrangements relevant to health care institutions, see Edward Lehman, *Coordinating Health Care* (Beverly Hills, California: Sage, 1975).

4. Sol Levine and Paul E. White, "Exchange as a Conceptual Framework for the Study of Interorganizational Relationships," *Administrative Science Quarterly* (March 1961), 5:503–601.

5. Eugene Litwak and L. F. Hylton, "Interorganizational Analysis: A Hypothesis on Coordinating Agencies," *Administrative Science Quarterly* (March 1962), 6:395–420.

6. Richard H. Hall et al., "Patterns of Interorganizational Relationships," *Administrative Science Quarterly* (September 1977), 22:457–73.

7. J. Kenneth Benson, "The Interorganizational Network as a Political Economy," *Administrative Science Quarterly* (June 1975), 20:229–49.

8. The material in the next two quotations has been made available through the courtesy of Barry Siegel.

9. Some large cities have relied on largely private profit-making ambulance services that have little or no centralized coordination. In some cases a terrible price may be paid. An informant who formerly worked in such a system operated by funeral homes claimed that ambulances would race each other to the scene of an accident. Purportedly, the winner would pick up the dead bodies, leaving the slower competitors the job of taking the injured to the hospital.

10. The process of referral transfer refers to the ambulance transport of a patient from one hospital to another by prior agreement for services the former hospital does not provide.

4. THE QUASI-MARKET IN PATIENT ALLOCATION

1. I do not mean to suggest that in the past Mercy refused to treat critically ill patients when they arrived at the emergency room. However, the vast majority of patients who come to a hospital emergency room are not critically ill in a life-or-death sense, and in the

past the amount of care that these patients could receive without paying for it was quite limited. It should be added that Mercy was probably more generous in this respect than most other voluntary hospitals.

2. Trauma refers to injuries caused by external objects and forces. For example, a crushed leg is a trauma case; a heart attack is not. Trauma cases commonly require surgery.

5. PARTICULARISTIC INTERACTION

1. The city ambulance service (CAS) and its central dispatch probably know that Johnson uses the ambulance for purposes other than emergency services, but neither Johnson nor CAS publicly admits this.

2. While institutions know that some times of the day, the week, or the year are likely to produce a much heavier demand for their services than others, precisely which institutions will be filled to maximum capacity at any given time is very unpredictable.

3. Peter M. Blau, *Exchange and Power in Social Life* (New York: Wiley, 1965), p. 141.

4. Peter M. Blau and W. Richard Scott, *Formal Organizations* (San Francisco: Chandler, 1962), pp. 217–21.

5. See Eugene Litwak and L. F. Hylton, "Interorganizational Analysis: A Hypothesis on Coordinating Agencies," *Administrative Science Quarterly* (March 1962), 6:395–420, for a discussion of the significance of standardization for interorganizational transactions. This is also compatible with the findings of the Aston group that there is a negative relationship between standardization (heavy reliance on universalistic roles) and centralization (that is, inequality of authority). Where standardization is feasible, less inequality is required—at least as a simplification mechanism. See Lex Donaldson et al., "The Aston Findings on Centralization: Further Discussion," *Administrative Science Quarterly* (September 1975), 20:453–60.

6. SYMBIOTIC INEQUALITY

1. Reinhard Bendix, *Max Weber* (Garden City, New York: Anchor Books, Doubleday, 1960), p. 331.

2. See Robert K. Merton, *Social Theory and Social Structure* (Glencoe, Ill.: Free Press, 1957), rev. ed., especially chaps. 8 and 9.

3. Jeffrey Pfeffer and Gerald R. Salancik, *The External Control of Organizations* (New York: Harper, 1978), chap. 6.

4. Gerhard E. Lenski, *Power and Privilege* (New York: McGraw-Hill, 1966), chap. 3.

5. Immanuel Wallerstein, *The Modern World-System* (New York: Academic Press, 1974).

7. INSTITUTIONAL CONTEXT

1. Some comments are required about the concepts of ideology and institutionalization. Ideology has a number of different senses; some are virtually contradictory. One common implication is that a set of ideas represents an attempt to make a case for the self-interests of

some subgroup, for example, "bourgeois ideology." A second, almost equally common implication is that the ideas are abstract, unrealistic, and illusory. Some combination of these two ideas is typical of the pejorative use of the term; some set of ideas is ideological rather than rational or scientific. This was a usage originated by Napoleon, to some degree taken up by Marx, and continued in contemporary sociology. (For two relatively recent discussions using the term primarily in this way, see Edward Shils, "Ideology," *International Encyclopedia of the Social Sciences* [New York: Macmillan, 1968], 7:66–76; and Lewis Feuer, *Ideology and the Ideologists* [New York: Harper Torch Books, 1975].) But ideology is also used in a more neutral and less pejorative sense; ideas are to some degree biased by the self-interest of the group holding them, but they are neither crass propaganda nor utopian irrationality. The Marxian tradition also includes this usage, for example, the notion of proletarian ideology. For a useful short discussion of the various meanings and usages, see Raymond Williams, *Key Words* (New York: Oxford University Press, 1976).

Since there is no generally agreed to meaning, all I can do is specify the meaning intended in this analysis. By ideology, I mean an idealized, and therefore to some degree abstract, statement of how things are "supposed to work." Such statements typically involve combinations of factual, normative, and value assertions. They are grounded in the point of view of some subgroup and are claimed to be valid for the group as a whole. The U.S. Chamber of Commerce's description of capitalism and the USSR Communist Party's description of socialism are to a significant degree ideological. But to some extent so are scientists' and philosophers' descriptions of how science operates—even those that stress conflict (e.g., Thomas Kuhn, *The Structure of Scientific Revolutions* [Chicago: University of Chicago Press, 1962]). Perhaps a good example of ideology in this sense is the official or formal organizational structures elaborated by the elite of an organization. The key notion is bias—typically unconscious—due to abstraction and parochial self-interest of the relevant subgroup. The primary connection between self-interest and bias is assumed to be selective perception. Obviously subgroups vary tremendously in the extent to which their interests are parochial and self-serving. In turn, this is reflected in their public descriptions of the ideal state of affairs. Moreover, tremendous variation occurs in how successful subgroups are in getting the broader group to accept their ideology as an appropriate description of how things should work, that is, in the extent to which an ideology has been institutionalized.

By "institutionalization" I mean that the idealized patterns are recognized as normative and are generally enforced. By "enforced" I mean that there is a high probability that an actor will be sanctioned for nonconformity to a specified pattern of behavior and that a large proportion of the population will permit, support, or participate in the sanctioning process. I do not mean that all or even a majority of the members of a given social system are direct advocates or supporters of a particular pattern of behavior, much less active enforcers. Often different interest groups take the lead in supporting a specific institutionalized pattern. For example, the dominant institutionalized pattern governing the payment for medical care has been fee-for-service. By no means is this institutionalized norm universally endorsed; obviously, its main support has come from the medical-profession. Nonetheless, until relatively recent years there has been a high probability that physicians who participated in other forms of financial arrangements would be sanctioned by their peers and that the other members of the society would at least tolerate the medical profession's enforcing this norm. Consequently, when I talk about institutionalized norms I simply mean that actors of a given type, in a specified social situation, are generally under pressure to conform to the described pattern of behavior and that these *pressures are rooted in a level of social organization more general than the relationships between the particular actors* that are the immediate focus of the analysis.

No assumption is made that the institutionalized norms are consistent, or, integrated. Contradictory institutionalized norms are not uncommon and often place actors in role conflict. In fact, one of the purposes of the analysis is to point out some of the contradictory institutionalized patterns.

The propositions used to describe the institutional context of urban health care are in a sense assumptions. The data collected for this study deal with only one small set of organizations. Therefore, the statements about the generalized institutionalized patterns of American society are not derived simply from the observations made during the case study. Rather, they are heavily dependent on general readings and impressionistic observations. By and large I believe that they are rather self-evident observations about American society. These assertions are introduced, not because they are original or because they are documented by systematic data, but because of a wish to make explicit the assumptions used to interpret the case study. It is hoped that this procedure will make it easier for the reader to understand the precise line of argument and judge for himself the validity of the assumptions and the analysis derived from them.

The use of institutionalized context in this analysis in many respects closely parallels Roland Warren's use of the concept of institutionalized thought structure (*The Structure of Urban Reform: Community Decision Organizations in Stability and Change* [Lexington, Massachusetts: Lexington Books, 1974]). However, Warren's concepts focus primarily on how thought patterns limit what people think about doing. The notion of institutionalized context is a broader concept that includes both Warren's notion and the sanctioning and social control processes that come into play when people deviate from the accepted norm.

A final caveat: obviously the notions of ideology and institutionalization have not been fully or systematically developed. I do not claim the conceptualization offered here as adequate for general theory but only as useful for the purpose at hand.

2. Charles Perrow, *Complex Organizations: A Critical Essay*, 2nd ed. (Glenview, Ill.: Scott, Foresman, 1979), chap. 5.

3. A. L. Stinchcombe, "Social Structure and Organizations," in James G. March, ed., *Handbook of Organizations* (Skokie, Ill.: Rand McNally, 1965), pp. 142–93.

4. John R. Kimberly, "Environmental Constraints and Organizational Structure: A Comparative Analysis of Rehabilitation Organizations," *Administrative Science Quarterly* (March 1975), 20:1–9.

5. Reinhard Bendix, *Work and Authority in Industry* (New York: Wiley, 1956).

6. John W. Meyer and Brian Rowan, "Institutionalized Organizations: Formal Structure as Myth and Ceremony," *American Journal of Sociology* (September 1977), 83:340–63.

7. Roland Warren et al., *The Structure of Urban Reform*.

8. Howard Aldrich, "Resource Dependence and Interorganizational Relations," *Administration and Society* (1976), 4:41–53; Richard H. Hall et al., "Patterns of Interorganizational Relationships," *Administrative Science Quarterly* (September 1977), 22:457–73; Jeffrey Pfeffer and Gerald R. Salancik, *The External Control of Organizations* (New York: Harper, 1978).

9. These differences are, of course, paralleled in the assumptions held about the appropriate means of controlling and using property. The market competition of capitalism assumes that most property will be privately owned, while society-wide planning and bureaucratic coordination assume extensive collective, that is, public, ownership.

10. See Charles Perrow, *Organizational Analysis: A Sociological View* (Belmont, Calif.:

Brooks/Cole, 1970), pp. 121–27, for a discussion of how businesses attempt to reduce uncertainty by suspending competition from time to time and even assisting competitors when they are hurt by disasters, etc.

11. John W. Meyer and Brian Rowan, "Institutionalized Organizations," pp. 340–63, have pointed out that the degree of divergence between formal structure and actual practice varies, but they have not explicitly noted that it varies by whole sectors of the economy.

12. This chain of command is clearest within the executive branch of the federal government, but in most cases relatively clear-cut procedures exist for resolving disputes and coordinating activities between the branches of the federal government and among the federal, state, and local governments. (When disputes between governmental agencies cannot be resolved by reference to a higher authority or a specified procedure, there is a "Constitutional crisis." These have been rare in the United States.) There may be less congruence between the actualities and the ideology for the governmental system than for the market system, but when one considers the extensiveness of the government, a high degree of conscious coordination by formal and explicit authority structures is evident.

13. The term is borrowed from John Kenneth Galbraith's *The New Industrial State* (Boston: Houghton-Mifflin, 1967). For a more extensive discussion of the relationship between the market system and the industrial system (which Galbraith has relabeled "the planning system"), see his newer book *Economics and the Public Purpose* (Boston: Houghton-Mifflin, 1973).

14. A few comments are in order about the boundaries of this system. First, the welfare system has a tendency to blur into the governmental sector. For example, some health care, many social services, and most education are provided by organizations supported and/or controlled by some unit of government. Nevertheless, compared to other nations, the United States has been slow to define health, education, and welfare services as the specific responsibility of the government. Hence, a large proportion of our welfare system is composed of nongovernmental organizations.

15. U.S. Department of Health, Education, and Welfare, *Towards a Systematic Analysis of Health Care in the United States: A Report to Congress* (Washington, D.C.: U.S. Government Printing Office, October 1972), p. 5. For a history of such complaints about the New York City health care system, see Robert Alford, *Health Care Politics: Ideological and Interest Group Barriers to Reform* (Chicago: University of Chicago Press, 1975), especially chap. 2.

16. Michael Aiken and Jerald Hage, "Organizational Interdependence and Intraorganizational Structure," in Merlin B. Brinkerhoff and Philip R. Kunz, eds., *Complex Organizations and Their Environments* (Dubuque, Iowa: Wm. C. Brown, 1972), pp. 367–94.

17. Burton R. Clark, "Interorganizational Patterns in Education," *Administrative Science Quarterly* (September 1965), 10:224–37; and Roland Warren, "The Interorganizational Field as a Focus for Investigation," *Administrative Science Quarterly* (December 1967), 12:396–419.

18. See Charles E. Lindblom, *The Intelligence of Democracy* (New York: Free Press, 1965), for a discussion of the efficiencies and inefficiencies of pluralistic decision-making. For a discussion of the stratification associated with pluralism, see William Domhoff and Hoyt B. Ballard, eds., *C. Wright Mills and the Power Elite* (Boston: Beacon Press, 1968); and Arnold M. Rose, *The Power Structure* (New York: Oxford University Press, 1967).

19. Alford, *Health Care Politics*, pp. 262–66; Roland Warren et al., *The Structure of Urban Reform*.

20. David Mechanic, *The Growth of Bureaucratic Medicine* (New York: Wiley, 1976), pp. 6off.

8. PLURALISTIC REFORM

1. Social conflict may frequently be a necessary prerequisite to integration of activity, but normally extensive severe conflict in the immediate situation reduces the possibility of interorganizational integration.

2. The "Four-Party Agreement" refers to the agreement between Mercy, the Southside Health Committee, the HCHC staff, and the city's health department, which supposedly specified the responsibilities and powers of each.

9. NEUTRALIZATION AND CONFLICT

1. Lewis Coser, *The Functions of Social Conflict* (New York: Free Press, 1956), p. 8.

2. *Ibid.*, pp. 48f.

3. Herman Turk, "Interorganizational Networks in Urban Society: Initial Perspectives and Comparative Research," *American Sociological Review* (February 1970), 35:1–19.

4. Robert P. Wolff et al., *Critique of Pure Tolerance* (Boston: Beacon, 1965).

5. Philip Selznick, *TVA and the Grassroots* (New York: Harper Torch Books, [1949], 1966).

6. Robert R. Alford, *Health Care Politics: Ideological and Interest Group Barriers to Reform* (Chicago: University of Chicago Press, 1975), p. 221.

7. Roland Warren et al., *The Structure of Urban Reform* (Lexington, Mass.: Lexington Books, 1974), p. 103.

8. *Ibid.*

9. Richard H. Hall et al., "Patterns of Interorganizational Relationships," *Administrative Science Quarterly* (September 1977), 22:457–73.

10. An influential conservative version of this theme is elaborated in Edward Banfield, *The Moral Basis of a Backward Society* (Glencoe, Ill.: Free Press, 1958). For a critique of Banfield's thesis, see William Muraskin, "The Moral Basis of a Backward Sociologist: Edward Banfield, the Italians, and the Italian-American," *American Journal of Sociology* (May 1974), 79:1484–96. For an analysis showing that illegal acts by an organization are related to the scarcity situation it faces, see Barry Staw and Eugene Stwajkowski, "The Scarcity-Munificence Component of Organizational Environments and the Commission of Illegal Acts," *Administrative Science Quarterly* (September 1975), 20:345–54.

11. J. Kenneth Benson, "The Interorganizational Network as a Political Economy," *Administrative Science Quarterly* (June 1975), 20:229–49. Benson also argues that positive evaluation will form part of this equilibrium, but as we shall see, our data do not fully support this conclusion.

12. For a discussion of the symbolic integrative function of boundary roles at the institutional level, see Peter Berger and Thomas Luckmann, *The Social Construction of Reality* (Garden City, N.Y.: Anchor Books, Doubleday, 1967), pp. 76f. At the level of a political constituency many politicians seek an image integrating a significant array of the conflicting interests among their constituents. For a discussion of a similar process for organizational executives, see Jeffrey Pfeffer and Gerald R. Salancik's discussion of executive succession,

The External Control of Organizations (New York: Harper, 1978), chap. 9; also see Gordon Baty et al., "Personnel Flows as Interorganizational Relations," *Administrative Science Quarterly* (December 1971), 16:430–43.

13. Max Weber, "Bureaucracy," *From Max Weber* (New York: Oxford University Press, 1947).

10. THE WELFARE STATE

1. T. H. Marshall, *Citizenship and Social Class* (Cambridge: University of Cambridge Press, 1950).

2. By "productive" I simply mean the ability of an individual to "earn his or her own way" according to the criteria and judgment of peers. It should also be kept in mind that the source of being nonproductive is less and less linked to physical incapacities. As we have shifted from an agrarian to an industrial economy, people are increasingly unable to earn their own way because of (1) the lack of demand for their labor—especially during recessions and depressions, (2) lack of sufficient training, or (3) discrimination against various ascribed characteristics such as race or sex. These are in turn at least in part related to a lack of access to the means of production as a larger and larger proportion of the work force has become wage laborers in the sense that they do not own the tools and resources needed to perform productive work.

3. Within the health field, the Health Policy Advisory Center (Health-PAC) has probably been the most enthusiastic advocate of community control. See, for example, Barbara and John Ehrenreich, *The American Health Empire: Power, Profits, and Politics* (New York: Vintage Books, Random House, 1970).

4. William C. Richardson, "Poverty, Illness, and the Use of Health Services in the United States," *Hospitals* (July 1969), 43:34–40; Philip M. Moody and Robert M. Gray, "Social Class, Social Integration and the Use of Preventive Health Services," in E. Gartly Jaco, ed., *Patients, Physicians and Illness* (New York: Free Press, 1972), pp. 250–61.

5. Edward A. Suchman, "Social Patterns of Illness and Medical Care," *Journal of Health and Human Behavior* (Spring 1965), 6:2–16; Leo Srole et al., *Mental Health in the Metropolis: The Midtown Manhattan Study* (New York: New York University Press, 1978).

6. The greater medical problems of the lower class can, of course, be overstated. See Charles Kadushin, "Social Class and Experience of Ill Health," *Sociological Inquiry* (Winter 1964), 34:67–80.

7. The notion of a more difficult-to-handle clientele is related to the concept of the "hardness of material." In industrial organizations it is recognized that "hard" materials are more difficult and costly to process. See W. A. Rushing, "Hardness of Material as Related to Division of Labor in Manufacturing Industries," *Administrative Science Quarterly* (September 1968), 13:229–45.

8. For more extended discussions of how the expansion of educational opportunities has not significantly affected class inequality, see my *The Illusion of Equality* (San Francisco: Jossey-Bass, 1972); Christopher Jencks et al., *Inequality* (New York: Basic Books, 1972); Ellen Kay Trimberger, "Open Admissions: A New Form of Tracking," *The Insurgent Sociologist* (Fall 1973), 4:29–43; Fred Pincus, "Tracking in Community Colleges," *The Insurgent Sociologist* (Spring 1974), 4:17–35.

9. For a cross-national analysis of the factors shaping the development of welfare mea-

sures, see Harold L. Wilensky, *The Welfare State and Equality* (Berkeley, Ca.: University of California Press, 1975). However, the quantitative parts of Wilensky's analysis have been severely criticized by Zald on methodological grounds. (See Meyer Zald's review of Wilensky's book, *American Journal of Sociology* [January 1977], 82:862–66). Moreover, while Wilensky's analysis is useful and provocative, it does not deal with the key issue being discussed here. Wilensky takes economic development and levels of wealth as independent variables and asks how they affect the welfare services offered by the state. My point is that the question must also be turned around; we need to ask to what extent our increased efficiency, wealth, and the availability of consumption goods are due to the fact that families and work units have been relieved of responsibility for the welfare function while the state has taken on the responsibility in only a halfhearted way. This is, of course, an old idea that goes back at least to Tocqueville. Alexis de Tocqueville, *Democracy in America*, Vol. II, chap. 20 (Garden City, N.Y.: Anchor Books, Doubleday, 1969), especially pp. 556–57.

10. *The Washington Post*, April 8, 1974. Nationwide figures from the American Hospital Association's *Hospital Statistics* indicate that for voluntary hospitals the percent of revenues going to bad debts, charity, and contractual adjustments were 5.7 percent in 1971, 6.5 percent in 1974, and 8.8 percent in 1977. They were undoubtedly much higher for hospitals close to urban ghettos.

11. It is important not to confuse the issue of being on welfare versus participating in production with the issue of whether one is in the official labor force, that is, sells one's labor in the market as a commodity. For example, the percentage of women employed in the official labor force has increased drastically. But when these women were "just housewives" they were very much a part of the total production process. Consequently, the shift of their productive activity from one location (the household) to another (the labor market) has relatively little significance for the issue of what percentage of the population are "on welfare" in the most basic sense of the concept.

12. There are, of course, some countervailing trends. Health, welfare, and rehabilitation services have enabled some people to be economically productive who could not have participated in the work of even the family farm or business. But this is more a matter of taking the increased production of the more standardized patterns of work and investing them in human capital, for example, physical therapy rehabilitation, to reduce ineptness. It does not negate the basic argument that it is harder for the inept and deviant to participate meaningfully in social production.

11. INTERPRETATIVE REPRISE

1. They may be partially transferable on the basis of stereotyping; Yale men may not be equally bright or trustworthy, but they do have some common set of experiences that in a high percentage of the cases simplify the establishment of acceptable mutual expectations between alumni who do not know one another. However, generalization based on broad social statuses can be misleading when complex specific behaviors must be predicted. A Yale man will probably behave appropriately if invited to your cocktail party, but it cannot be assumed that he will vote for the candidate you support.

2. There is a debate within the sociological literature over the positive and negative effects of ascription. See Theodore D. Kemper, "On the Nature and Purpose of Ascription," *American Sociological Review* (December 1974), 39:844–53; Leon Mayhew and John Finley

Scott, "Cui Bono (Comment on Kemper)," and Theodore D. Kemper, "Reply to Mayhew and Scott," *American Sociological Review* (April 1976), 41:386–89. From the perspective of the discussion presented here, the debate over the functional versus conflict interpretations of ascription is in part due to a confusion between the effects of ascription and the simplification effects of particularism. At least some of the functional contributions assigned to ascription are more adequately seen as the simplifying effects of particularistic relations rather than ascription per se. Other theoretical discussions that touch on these issues include the discussions of typifications by Peter Berger and Thomas Luckmann, *The Social Construction of Reality* (Garden City, New York: Doubleday, 1966) and the discussion of communication competence by Jurgen Habermas, "Toward a Theory of Communication Competence," *Recent Sociology No. 2*, Hans Peter Dreitzel, ed. (New York: Macmillan Co., 1970).

3. Sol Levine and Paul E. White, "Exchange as a Conceptual Framework for the Study of Interorganizational Relationships," *Administrative Science Quarterly* (March 1961), 5:583–601; J. Kenneth Benson, "The Interorganizational Network as a Political Economy," *Administrative Science Quarterly* (June 1975), 20:229–49.

4. Roland Warren et al., *The Structure of Urban Reform* (Lexington, Mass.: Lexington Books, 1974).

5. Benson, "Interorganizational Network."

6. Howard Aldrich, "Resource Dependence and Interorganizational Relations," *Administration and Society* (1976), 4:419–53.

7. Warren et al., *Structure of Urban Reform*.

8. A few words are needed about the concept of stratification system. The term can be used to refer to all structures of social inequality tending to persist over time, including formal authority structures such as bureaucracies and modern governments. In this context I use a more restricted definition referring to relatively informal systems of inequality not involving formal authority relationships. The asymmetry in such systems involves primarily deference to wealth, prestige, and influence, rather than submission to formal authority. This is admittedly not a precise distinction, but it is satisfactory for the purposes at hand. On the other hand, some definitions of stratification systems emphasize individuals and families as the unit of analysis and focus on intergenerational transmission of power, privilege, and prestige. The concept used here is obviously broader, since our focus is on organizations rather than families.

9. We are referring to the distribution of power between the interorganizational actors within each subsystem. This is not to assume anything about the distribution of power between the subsystems, for example, the relative ability of the industrial system to influence the government system or vice versa.

10. Informal structure is a long-discussed concept in organizational analysis. Peter Blau has emphasized that departures from formal structures are not necessarily intended to subvert organizational goals but are often intended as innovations to improve organizational performance. See *The Dynamics of Bureaucracy*, rev. ed. (Chicago: University of Chicago Press, 1963).

11. In this context "legitimate" is used in a very weak sense. It does not mean that the expectations of the first actor are generally seen as legitimate by third parties. Rather, it simply means that the first party feels justified, politically if not morally, in using negative sanctions.

12. I do not mean to imply that this is necessarily the way Pfeffer and Salancik themselves would analyze the data I have presented. I am suggesting, however, that the kinds of

analyses that I outline can be implied from the logical structure of their theoretical perspective presented in *The External Control of Organizations* (New York: Harper, 1978).

13. Gerhard E. Lenski, *Power and Privilege* (New York: McGraw-Hill, 1966).

14. Donald Treiman, *Occupational Prestige in Comparative Perspective* (New York: Academic Press, 1977). On the other hand, Treiman overstates the universality of occupational prestige ratings. See Archibald Haller and David B. Bills, "Occupational Prestige Hierarchies: Theory and Evidence," *Contemporary Sociology* (September 1979), 8:721–34. Moreover, the theoretical argument behind Treiman's observations is, to say the least, debatable.

15. Immanuel Wallerstein, *The Modern World-System* (New York: Academic Press, 1974).

16. Max Weber, "Bureaucracy," *From Max Weber* (New York: Oxford University Press, 1947).

INDEX

Responsible administration, 121; and scarcity, 123-25
Rewards: achievement, equality, and distributive justice, 138-42
Rhetoric, *see* Ideology
Richardson, William C., 190
Rights of citizenship, expansion of, 139-40
Role conflict: and boundary personnel, 125-27; for institutions, 133; and welfare cheating, 153; *see also* Boundary personnel; Conflict
Rose, Arnold M., 188
Rowan, Brian, 82, 187, 188
Rushing, W. A., 190

Salancik, 11, 30, 77, 171, 185, 187, 189, 192
Satellite programs: effect on allocation of patients, 129-30; and community participation, 142-43; as reasonable reform strategy, 146
Satellite relationships and links, 94-97; as mandated diffuse linkage, 119-20; reasons for participation in, 127-28
Scarcity: and resource dependency, 10-12; reduction through production, 11; and particularism, 123-25, 158; and "playing the averages," 124
School desegregation: and interorganizational inequality, 147; and pluralism, 149
Scott, John Finley, 191-92
Scott, W. Richard, 64, 185
Selznick, Philip, 13, 116, 182, 189
Services, secured by farming-out system, 50-57
Setting of the study, description of, 16-17
Sharing equipment and staff, HCHC-City health department, 96, 99
SHC (pseudonym), *see* Southside Health Committee
Shils, Edward, 183, 186
Siegel, Barry, 181, 184
Simplification: abstraction and inequality as basic mechanisms of, 28-29; by markets, 38; by abstractions, 38; universalistic rules, 66-67; particularistic relations, 67-68; universalism and particularism as alternatives, 68; inequality as simplification mechanisms, 70; by particularistic relations, 156-60; relation to stratification,

162; by bastardized mechanisms, 164; relation to dominance, 178; *see also* Decision-making; Simplification mechanisms
Simplification mechanisms, 28-29; unavailability of, 119; *see also* Simplification
Sit-ins: at Mercy Hospital, 44; at HCHC to protest secretary's firing, 103
Size of institution, and empire building, 130
Social change, *see* Change
Social inequality, *see* Inequality
Socialism, 83-86
Social order, 155
Society, productive and nonproductive members of, 140-41; concept of, 190; relation to labor force participation, 191
Sorting, of patients, *see* Allocation of patients
Southside (pseudonym), *see* Setting of the study
Southside Health Committee (SHC) (pseudonym), 44, 93, 100-11; reorganization of, 105
Spanish-speaking ghetto and Johnson hospital, 18; patients of HCHC, 91
Specialization, of health care, 20
Specialty clinics, as a back-up service, 96
Srole, Leo, 190
Stability: of established relations, 156-57; of structures of inequality, 177-79
Staff accreditation, at HCHC, 95
Stalemate, 8; *see also* Neutralization
Standardization: of cases and centralized authority, 34-35; of commodities, 38; and abstractions, 38; and universalistic rules, 67-68, 156; and interorganizational relations, 185
Status anxiety, and interorganizational cooperation, 64-5
Staw, Barry, 189
Stratification: dual nature of, 79; concept of, 192; *see also* Inequality; Symbolic inequality
Stratification theory, 172-74, 176-77
Stinchcombe, A. L., 82, 187
Strauss, Anselm, 183
Structural features: market imperfections as non-erratic, 39; in contrast to personality problems, 114